CATULLUS

ADVANCED PLACEMENT* EDITION

Student Text

by

Henry V. Bender, Ph.D.

St. Joseph's Preparatory School and Villanova University

and

Phyllis Young Forsyth, Ph.D.

University of Waterloo

Bolchazy-Carducci Publishers, Inc.
Wauconda, Illinois USA

*AP is a registered trademark of the College Entrance Examination Board,
which was not involved in the production of, and does not endorse, this product.

Contributing editor:
Thalia Pantelidis Hocker

General editor:
Laurie Haight Keenan

Cover illustration:
Girl with pigeons, fifth century B.C.
Athenian grave stele, Metropolitan Museum, New York

Cover design:
Bensen Studios

Bolchazy-Carducci Publishers, Inc.
1000 Brown Street, Unit 101
Wauconda, Illinois 60084

http://www.bolchazy.com

Printed in the United States of America
by United Graphics
2002
ISBN 0-86516-275-1

Library of Congress Cataloging-in-Publication Data

Catullus, Gaius Valerius.
   [Selections.   1996]
   Catullus : student text / [edited] by Henry V. Bender and Phyllis
Young Forsyth. -- Advanced placement ed.
   p.   cm.
   Summary: Includes an introduction to this Roman poet, selections
from his poetry, vocabulary and grammatical notes, and glossaries on
meters and figures of speech.
   ISBN 0-86516-275-1 (alk. paper)
   1. Love poetry, Latin. 2. Epigrams, Latin. 3. Rome--Poetry.
[1. Love--Poetry. 2. Epigrams. 3. Rome--Poetry.] I. Bender,
Henry V., 1945-   . II. Forsyth, Phyllis Young. III. Title.
PA6274.A25   1996
871'.01--dc21
                                        96-43616
                                        CIP
                                        AC

Contents

Preface

This book is the result of twelve years of teaching the Advanced Placement* syllabus. Its goal is to assist and encourage the initial efforts of upper level high school or intermediate level college readers of Catullus to comprehend the poems which comprise the Advanced Placement* syllabus.

There are many texts of Catullus which supply excellent scholarly commentary—such as those of Garrison, Quinn, and Merrill. But I have always found it necessary to supplement what these authors say in order to make the grammar, vocabulary, and themes of the poetry readily accessible for my busy and pressured students.

The *Teacher's Manual* features, with minor orthographic changes, the Latin text established by Mynors (Oxford 1958). The poems in the *Teacher's Manual* are printed in large type so that they can be duplicated for distribution in class or made into overhead transparencies for review or sight work in class. Such use permits fast review, prevents the student from constant dependence upon vocabulary glosses, and provides an easy text for testing and poem contrast or analysis. Literal, prose translations of each poem are offered, and tests which address grammar, figures of speech, syntax, and interpretative issues. The format of these tests replicates the format of the A.P.* examination. Teachers can configure these sample tests to suit their own needs. Finally, a select bibliography is appended.

The *Student Text* begins with an introduction on what we know of Catullus' life and background, essentially the foundation for reading the A.P.* selections. A brief head note introduces the text of each poem which is followed by notes and vocabulary. A glossed vocabulary word will appear beside its line number as that word appears in the text of the poem. Next to this entry, the basic form or forms from which the word has been derived are presented. Verbs (except for deponents) have their fourth part in *-um;* all adjectives are listed with their nominative singular forms fitting the patterns *-us-a-um* or *-is-e,* etc. Meters are identified with full explanation appearing in a separate appendix. A glossary of figures of speech with examples drawn from poems under study likewise appears as an appendix. Finally, there is a dictionary of Catullan vocabulary words used throughout the text.

These textbooks should not be expected to do everything for everybody, but they have been effective in whetting the appetite of students to go on with Latin studies, and to achieve a strong toehold in the syntax and vocabulary of Roman lyric poetry. I would like to express my thanks to the many students of mine who worked through this material with me over my many years at St. Joseph's Prep, as well as to my colleagues at schools who so gener-

*AP is a registered trademark of the College Entrance Examination Board, which was not involved in the production of, and does not endorse, this product.

ously have given suggestions and time to me as they used various versions of these texts in earlier forms. These schools include the Baldwin School, Boston College High School, the Hill School, St. Joseph's Prep, the Lawrenceville School, Mount Saint Joseph Academy, North Penn High School, Oratory Prep School, the Westminster School, and Xavier Preparatory School.

I am pleased to acknowledge the special enthusiasm of Thalia Hocker for this project, and the fine fruit born of her enthusiasm. She spent considerable time and effort on re-formatting the *Student Text* to make it much more user-friendly than it originally was. Another special thank-you goes to one of my students at St. Joseph's Preparatory School, Malachy Egan, whose line drawings based on ancient originals add pleasant decoration to the text.

I was most fortunate in obtaining the help of Professor Phyllis Young Forsyth, who agreed to be my co-author as I faced the formidable task of turning a working, classroom text into one that could be of as much use as possible to our colleagues. Professor Forsyth's many suggestions and corrections throughout both the *Student Text* and *Teacher's Manual*, along with her complete revisions of the introduction and bibliography, are welcome additions to my own work.

Henry V. Bender, Ph.D.
St. Joseph's Preparatory School
and Villanova University
Philadelphia, PA
August, 1996

An Introduction to Catullus

Catullus: The Historical Context

Gaius Valerius Catullus (ca. 84–54 B.C.) lived during one of the most turbulent periods in Roman history. The first century B.C., (the last century of the Roman Republic) saw a breakdown of government as ambitious and powerful generals commanded legions more loyal to themselves than to the state. Only about four years before the birth of the poet the Roman general Sulla had led his troops in a march on Rome itself, and in 60 B.C., when Catullus was still in his twenties, Julius Caesar, Pompey the Great, and Marcus Crassus formed the First Triumvirate, an illegal pact designed to take control of the Roman government. As would-be rulers like Caesar and Pompey usurped the powers of the Roman Senate, Republican loyalists like the great orator Cicero could do little to turn back the clock. It was only a matter of time until Caesar and Pompey would engage in a civil war that would end in the triumph of the former and the total collapse of the Republican constitution. It was against this unsettled and violent background that Catullus created the poems that we have today, some of which in fact allude to the politics and politicians of the day.

The Life of Catullus

Very little is actually known about the life of Catullus, although a close reading of his poems offers some biographical data. The poems and other ancient sources indicate that he was born in the northern town of Verona, in what was then known as Cisalpine Gaul, and that his family was prominent enough to associate with Julius Caesar himself. It is likely that Catullus moved from Verona to Rome as a young man, not to pursue a career in politics, as might be expected of a scion of an important family, but rather to enjoy the more cosmopolitan atmosphere of the capital. In Rome Catullus soon met many people whose names appear in his poems, such as the lawyer, writer, and orator Cicero, the promising young politician Caelius Rufus, and the lawyer and poet Licinius Calvus. In short order, Catullus concentrated his attention on poetry and became a member of the so-called Neoterics (or "New Poets"), a circle of men who brought to the Roman literature of their time a new infusion of Greek, or, more specifically, Alexandrian (so-called after the city of Alexandria in Egypt) poetic principles. The Neoterics were especially influenced by the Greek Alexandrian poet Callimachus (ca. 310–240 B.C.), who had advocated the writing of short, but elegant and very learned poems. It is illustrative of Catullus' admiration for Callimachus that his Poem 66 is a close translation of a poem by that Alexandrian author. While other Greek poets also influenced the Neoterics (e.g., Poem 51 of Catullus is for the most part a translation of a Greek poem by the renowned Sappho of Lesbos), none had as great an impact as Callimachus. In the particular case of Catullus, Callimachus' great concern for learning and form would become merged with the Roman poet's own passion and wit to create a type of poetry unique in Rome. [For an examination of the Neoteric movement in general, see R. O. A. M. Lyne's "The Neoteric Poets" in the *Classical Quarterly* 28 (1978) 167–187.]

While Catullus clearly associated with some of the best young poets of the day, by far the most famous acquaintance he made in Rome was Clodia, a woman of great intelligence, wit, and beauty who became immortalized in his poems under the pseudonym of

"Lesbia" (a name chosen in order to associate Clodia with the equally unique Sappho of Lesbos, both women being *docta*, that is, highly cultured and educated). Most modern scholars believe that Catullus' Clodia was the wife of Quintus Metellus Celer, a conservative Roman aristocrat who had served as governor of Cisalpine Gaul in 62–61 B.C.; some even theorize that Catullus had first met Clodia in Cisalpine Gaul and then had followed her to Rome. This worldly woman was a member of a politically influential Roman family, and her brother, Publius Clodius, played a role in the downfall of the Republic as an amoral thug-for-hire. Clodia, who was at least ten years older than Catullus, enchanted the young poet, and their affair would inspire some of the finest poems in the Catullan collection. Catullus even seems to have looked upon their liaison as a form of marriage, and he may have hoped that, with the death of Metellus in 59 B.C., Clodia would actually marry him. If so, he was to be extremely disappointed, since Clodia not only did not reciprocate Catullus' passion, but even took a new lover in the person of Caelius Rufus.

To the everlasting delight of historians, Clodia's affair with Caelius came to a disastrous end which was well documented by Cicero in his *Pro Caelio*. Caelius must have come to realize that his liaison with Clodia would not help advance his political career in Rome, and so he seems to have ended their relationship. Clodia, however, was not a woman to take rejection lightly: in 56 B.C. she filed charges against Caelius, accusing him of the act of *vis* (that is, extreme political violence) and of attempting to murder her. In response, Caelius turned to Cicero to defend him. The result was the famous speech *Pro Caelio*, in which Cicero completely destroyed the credibility of Clodia. Unfortunately, how Catullus reacted to the scandal surrounding both his friend and his lover is not clear.

Not surprisingly, discussions of the complex relationship between Catullus and Clodia have been the focus of much modern secondary literature. Perhaps the most thorough and at the same time most provocative analysis can be found in T. P. Wiseman's *Catullus and His World: A Reappraisal* (Cambridge, 1985). As for Clodia, an excellent article is that of M. B. Skinner, "Clodia Metelli" in the *Transactions of the American Philological Association* 113 (1983) 273–287. See also A. L. Wheeler, *Catullus and the Traditions of Ancient Poetry* (Berkeley, 1934), and G. P. Goold, *Catullus* (London, 1983).

As difficult as the loss of Clodia must have been, another great loss also deeply affected Catullus: the unexpected death of his brother in the Troad of Asia Minor ca. 59 B.C. One of the best known Catullan poems (101) refers to this loss, and suggests that the poet eventually went to the Troad to make funerary offerings at his brother's grave. Many scholars have argued that this trip and the ensuing poem date to the period 57–56 B.C., when Catullus joined the general staff of Gaius Memmius, the new governor of the eastern province of Bithynia. On his return home, Catullus seems to have spent some time at his villa at Sirmio in northern Italy (the modern Lake Garda). Shortly thereafter Catullus died, probably at the relatively young age of thirty. Like so many other details of Catullus' life, the cause of his death remains unknown.

The Poems of Catullus

The collection of over 100 poems that forms the Catullan corpus is colored dramatically by the poems to and about Lesbia. These poems depict the growth, maturity, and dissolution of a complex relationship, but are nonetheless far more than spontaneous outbursts of love and/or hate. While Catullus is often (and to some degree rightly) praised for his explosive candor and depth of feeling in the so-called "Lesbia poems," he was at all times a consummate artist, conscious of his audience and of literary tradition. The genius of Catullus indeed lies in the fact that he successfully employed studied artistry in the expression of intense emotions that still affect readers to this day.

It is important to realize that, despite their prominence in the eyes of modern readers, the Lesbia poems represent only one aspect of a larger collection. Catullus often turned his attention to other subjects, and among his poems are many which deal in one way or another with friendship. The poet seems to have expected from his friends the same kind of loyalty he wished for in vain from Lesbia: those who remained his steadfast friends, men such as Veranius, Calvus, or Fabullus, find their reward in poems that express genuine affection, while those who betrayed the trust of the poet find themselves the recipients of vilifying poems such as 73. Indeed, the breaking of trust in general seems to lie behind the harshest invectives to be found in the collection.

Literary themes (e.g., what is good or bad writing) infuse many poems (e.g., 1, 22, 35, 36, 44, 50). A close reading of these poems reveals Catullus' deep respect both for the power of the written word and for the art of transforming words into poetry. Poem 50 is especially instructive in providing the reader with a window into the world of poetic composition: we watch carefully as Catullus and his friend Calvus compete with each other in the making of poetry. From such poems we gain valuable insight into Catullus as a Neoteric, "Callimachean" poet who extols the virtue of quality over quantity and praises substance over image.

Other themes of note in the Catullan collection include marriage (especially dominant in poems 61–68), travel (e.g., 4 , 11, 46), and bad manners or habits (e.g., 10, 12, 84). From the collection as a whole, in fact, we come to understand the world of Catullus—his likes and dislikes, his friends and enemies, his values, and, not least in importance, his views on the art of poetry itself.

The "Book" of Catullus

Did Catullus arrange his poems in the order in which we have them today ? This question has occupied much scholarship over the years. The first poem in the collection, the dedication of Catullus' book to Cornelius Nepos, uses the Latin word *libellus*, a diminutive form which may simply express humility on the part of the poet, or which may indeed indicate that only a small collection of poems had been made. For a long time scholars were convinced that the collection as we have it was the work of a later editor, but more recent scholarship has suggested that at least parts of the collection do reflect the ordering intended by Catullus.

A "minimalist" position takes the view that only poems 1–14 constituted the *libellus* of Catullus [cf. T. K. Hubbard, "The Catullan Libellus," *Philologus* 127 (1983) 218–237]. At the opposite end of the critical spectrum, T. P. Wiseman has argued that the entire collection as we have it (1–116) was arranged and published by the poet himself [cf. T. P. Wiseman, *Catullan Questions* (Leicester, 1969); see also J. D. Minyard, "The Source of the Catulli Veronensis Liber," *Classical World* 81 (1988) 343–353]. In between these extremes are "moderates" who see the *libellus* as consisting of poems 1–51 [cf. M. B. Skinner, *Catullus' Passer: The Arrangement of the Book of Polymetric Poems* (New York, 1981)], or perhaps of poems 1–60 [cf.

Kenneth Quinn, *Catullus: The Poems* (London, 1970); also, W. Clausen, "Catulli Veronensis Liber," *Classical Philology* 71 (1976) 37–43]. Given the lack of conclusive evidence, readers of the poems are encouraged to form their own opinions on this matter.

Whatever Catullus' original *libellus* was, the text as we have it today falls clearly into three sections arranged by meter and length: poems 1–60 (known as the poly-metrics) are short pieces composed in a variety of lyric meters, the most common being the hendecasyllabic; the more expansive poems 61–68 are classified as the "long poems"; and poems 69–116 are epigrams written in the elegiac meter. The very existence of these three categories demonstrates the versatility of Catullus as a poet: he was not bound to any single type of verse, but preferred to experiment in several. It is hoped that the selection of poems made here will enable the student of Catullus to appreciate his genius as a poet who was able to unite artistry with passion in a way few others have ever achieved.

CATULLUS

Advanced Placement Edition

[Blue] = FS

<u>Black</u> = C + R

<u>Green</u> = Syntax (identify type of verb form)

Black (boxed) = degree of comparison (adj / adv)

Red = explain 2 significant facts

1

Catullus probably wrote this poem when he was finished writing his collection. But what was that collection? We do not know exactly what he refers to by the word *libellus*. The 116 poems of Catullus are divisible into three groups: the polymetric poems 1–60, the long poems 61–68, and the elegiac distich poems 69–116. There is ample justification for thinking that the collection which we possess is a merging of several *libelli*. But there is considerable question as to where the separation of lines is or was, and further, whether we have the poems in the order in which the poet wanted them arranged. Poems 1–3 are in the hendecasyllabic meter.

> Cui dono lepidum novum libellum
> arida modo pumice expolitum?
> Corneli, tibi: namque tu solebas
> meas esse aliquid putare nugas
> iam tum, cum ausus es unus Italorum   5
> omne aevum tribus explicare cartis
> doctis, Iuppiter, et laboriosis.
> quare habe tibi quidquid hoc libelli
> qualecumque; quod, <o> patrona virgo,
> plus uno maneat perenne saeclo.   10

---

1   dono: **dono, donare, donavi, donatum**, give, dedicate
    cui: (interrogative pronoun) to whom?
    lepidum: **lepidus-a-um**, adj., fine, elegant, charming
        Does the poet refer here to a physical attribute of the finished book
        itself?
    libellum: **libellus, -i**, m., small book; it is important to
        observe the way in which the poet uses alliteration and
        diminutives. What special effects does this word produce?

2   arida: **aridus-a-um**, adj., dry
    modo: **modo**, adv., just, now, only recently
    pumice: **pumex, pumicis**, m./f., lava-stone, pumice
    expolitum: **expolio, expolire, expolivi, expolitum,**
        smooth off, polish; this book originally would have been written onto sheets made from
        strips of the papyrus plant. The uneven seams created by the bonding of one piece of
        papyrus with another by means of the natural secretions released in stripping the plant
        itself would require the use of pumice stone to gently smooth the papyrus into a scroll.

3   Corneli: vocative form of the proper noun **Cornelius**; this is Cornelius Nepos, author of a
        tersely written history whose learnedness and polish won the admiration of Catullus.
    nam: **nam**, conj., for, with the enclitic conjunction **que**
    solebas: **soleo, solere, solitus sum**, be accustomed to (with a complementary infinitive)

4   aliquid: **aliquis-aliquid**, (indefinite pronoun)
        someone, something
    putare: **puto, putare, putavi, putatum**, think, consider
    nugas: **nugae, -arum**, f. (plural), nothings, nonsense, trifles

5   **ausus es: audeo, audere, ausus sum**, dare
    unus: unus-a-um, adj., alone, one

6   **aevum: aevum, aevi**, n., age, history
    tribus: tres-tres-tria, adj., three
    explicare: explico, explicare, explicavi, explicatum
        unfold, explain; does **explicatum** recall **expolitum** of line 2?
    cartis: carta, cartae, f., a sheet of the Egyptian papyrus;
        cartae suggests a series of sheets glued together to form a scroll, hence
        three volumes.

7   **doctis: doceo, docere, docui, doctum**, teach; the perfect passive participle used here means
        "learned."
    Iuppiter: (vocative case, an apostrophe) Jupiter. The poet may be invoking the king of the
        gods to emphasize his admiration for Cornelius' literary accomplishments.
    laboriosis: laboriosus-a-um, adj., labored over, worked

8   **quare: quare**, adv., on account of which thing; therefore
    habe tibi: an abrupt, colloquial phrase with legalistic overtones suggesting the transfer of
        real property; essentially Catullus says, "Take it in 'as-is' condition."
    quidquid: quisquis-quaequae-quidquid, (substantive use of the indefinite relative pronoun)
        whoever, whatever

9   **qualecumque: qualiscumque-qualecumque,**
        (interrogative/indefinite adjective) of whatever sort
    quod: qui, quae, quod, (relative pronoun), refers to a neuter indefinite antecedent which is
        the object of the imperative **habe** and modified by **qualecumque.**
    <o>: Pointed brackets like these indicate an omission in the original
        manuscript which has been tentatively restored by the text editor to complete the meter.
    patrona: patronus/a, -i/ae, m./f., patron
    virgo: virgo, virginis, f., maiden, virgin; with the words **patrona virgo**, the poet is invoking
        a muse in a manner which recalls the invocation of the muse in Homer.

10   **plus: plus**, adv., (followed by ablative of comparison) more
    maneat: maneo, manere, mansi, mansum, remain; here the jussive subjunctive form means
        "let it remain."
    perenne: perennis-perenne, adj., enduring, unending
    saeclo: saeclum, saecli, n., an age, a generation

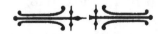

2

The occasion of this poem, the first of the *passer* poems, is the poet's fanciful jealousy of a pet sparrow. The sparrow has been fortunate to become the focus of the attention of Catullus' girlfriend, Lesbia (Clodia). This occasion makes the poet eager to be with his beloved, to play with the sparrow and to receive the love and attention he craves.

> Passer, deliciae meae puellae,
> quicum ludere, quem in sinu tenere,
> cui primum digitum dare appetenti
> et acris solet incitare morsus,
>
> cum desiderio meo nitenti   5
> carum nescio quid lubet iocari,
> et solaciolum sui doloris,
> credo, ut tum gravis acquiescat ardor:
> tecum ludere sicut ipsa possem
> et tristis animi levare curas!   10

---

1   **passer: passer, passeris**, m., sparrow
   deliciae: deliciae, deliciarum, f. (plural), delight, favorite, "sweetheart"

2   **quicum = quocum:** (relative pronoun) with whom
   ludere: ludo, ludere, lusi, lusum, play
   sinu: sinus, sinus, m., the fold of the toga at the breast or chest, one's lap
   tenere: teneo, tenere, tenui, tentum, hold, keep

3   **cui:** (relative pronoun) to whom
   digitum: digitus, digiti, m., finger
 * **primum digitum:** fingertip of the index finger
   appetenti: appeto, appetere, appetivi, appetitum, seek, seek greedily

4   **acris: acer-acris-acre**, adj., sharp, fierce
   solet: soleo, solere, solitus sum, be accustomed to, be used to; this verb takes four complementary infinitives, **ludere, tenere, dare, incitare**.
   morsus: morsus, morsus, m., hunger pain, a bite, a peck

5   **cum: cum**, conj., when
   desiderio: desiderium, desiderii, n., longing
   nitenti: niteo, nitere, nitui, shine, be bright; the participle may be modifying the noun **desiderio** or may be taken with an unexpressed but understood word for Lesbia in the dative case. **Desiderio** would then be taken as an ablative qualifying **nitenti**, and **meo**, while strictly speaking a possessive adjective, can be taken in the sense of "for me."

6   **nescio: nescio, nescire, nescivi**, not know: with the indefinite pronoun **quis-quid**, an indefinite idiomatic adjectival construction modifying **carum**, and with **iocari** it means "to make some loving joke."
   lubet = libet: libet, libere, libuit/libitum est, it pleases
   iocari: iocor, iocari, iocatus sum, tease, joke

7   **solaciolum: solaciolum, solacioli**, n., a little comfort or solace
   doloris: dolor, doloris, m., grief, pain

8   **credo: credo, credere, credidi, creditum**, believe
   gravis: gravis-grave, adj., serious, dire, grave
   acquiescat: acquiesco, acquiescere, acquievi, acquietum, become quiet, settle down
   ardor: ardor, ardoris, m., flame of passion

9   **sicut: sicut**, conj., just as
   possem: possum, posse, potui, (optative subjunctive) be able

10   **tristis: tristis-triste**, adj., sad, miserable. This is an example of the poetic form of the regular third declension accusative plural ending, **-es**.
   animi: animus, animi, m., mind, being
   levare: levo, levare, levavi, levatum, lighten
   curas: cura, curae, f., care, anxiety, love

2B

Some scholars have suggested that several lines are missing at the end of Poem 2. They believe that these missing lines would have formed a coherent connection with Poem 2b.

> tam gratum est mihi 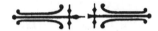quam ferunt puellae
> pernici aureolum fuisse malum,
> quod zonam soluit diu ligatam.

1   **gratum est:** it is pleasing
   ferunt: in the sense of "they say"
   puellae: refers to Atalanta, who was to marry the person who surpassed her in running. Milanion dropped a golden apple in front of Atalanta while racing her. She stopped to pick up the apple and was thereby defeated by Milanion, who then won her hand in marriage.

2   **pernici: pernix, pernicis**, adj., swift
   aureolum: aureolus-a-um, adj., golden
   malum: malum, -i, n., apple

3   **zonam: zona, -ae**, f., girdle
   solvit: solvo, solvere, solvi, solutum, free up, untie
   ligatam: ligo, ligare, ligavi, ligatum, tie up, bind

3

The second sparrow poem paints a semi-serious picture of Catullus inviting his listeners to cry with him over the death of the little sparrow, a virtual mock funeral. The poem builds considerable pathos for the deceased sparrow, and offers a dramatic tonal contrast with Poem 2.

Lugete, O Veneres Cupidinesque,
et quantum est hominum venustiorum:
passer mortuus est meae puellae,
passer, deliciae meae puellae,
quem plus illa oculis suis amabat.   5
nam mellitus erat suamque norat
ipsam tam bene quam puella matrem,
nec sese a gremio illius movebat,
sed circumsiliens modo huc modo illuc
ad solam dominam usque pipiabat;   10
qui nunc it per iter tenebricosum
illud, unde negant redire quemquam.
at vobis male sit, malae tenebrae
Orci, quae omnia bella devoratis:
tam bellum mihi passerem abstulistis.   15
O factum male! O miselle passer!
tuā nunc operā meae puellae
flendo turgiduli rubent ocelli.

---

1   lugete: **lugeo, lugere, luxi, luctum**, mourn, lament

2   quantum: **quantus-a-um**, (interrogative adj.) how much; used here as a pronoun upon which
        the subsequent genitives depend.
     venustiorum: **venustus-a-um**, adj., beautiful, charming. Note that this form is the genitive
        plural of the comparative degree of **venustus**, which modifies **hominum**, a genitive of
        the whole or partitive genitive.

5   plus: **plus, pluris**, adj., more
     illa: **ille-illa-illud**, (demonstrative pronoun/adjective) that;
        illa: nominative case, subject of the verb **amabat**, effectively an emphatic personal pro-
        noun meaning she.
     oculis: **oculus, -i**, m., eye; **oculis** is an ablative of comparison introduced by **plus**. Note the
        figure of speech, chiasmus.

6   mellitus: **mellitus-a-um**, adj., honey-sweet
     norat = noverat: syncopated pluperfect active form
     norat: **nosco, noscere, novi, notum**, know, be acquainted with

7   **ipsam: ipse-ipsa-ipsum,** (intensive pronoun) -self; here **ipsam** is probably being used as a noun to stand for the words, "the lady herself, the lady in charge, the mistress"; essentially **ipsam = dominam.**

8   **gremio: gremium, -ii,** n., lap

9   **circumsiliens: circumsilio, circumsilire,** hop around

10   **pipiabat: pipio, pipiare** or **pipire, pipiavi, pipiatum,** chirp

11   **qui:** (relative pronoun) refers to **passer**
      tenebricosum: tenebricosus-a-um, adj., dark, obscure, murky

12   **quemquam: quisquam-quidquam,** (indefinite pronoun) anyone, anybody, any person

13   **sit:** may it be, may it go (jussive subjunctive)
      male: male, adv., badly
      tenebrae: tenebrae, -arum, f., (plural) darkness (of the underworld)

14   **Orci: Orcus, -i,** m., name of the god of the underworld, metonymy for the entire underworld
      devoratis: devoro, devorare, devoravi, devoratum, devour, destroy
      bella: bellus-a-um, adj., beautiful, nice. Note apostrophe, personification, and chiasmus in this line.

15   **mihi:** (dative of separation) from me
      abstulistis: aufero, auferre, abstuli, ablatum, take away, steal

16   **miselle: misellus-a-um,** adj., poor little (diminutive form of the adjective **miser-misera-miserum**)

17   **opera: opera, -ae,** f., work, deed

18   **flendo: fleo, flere, flevi, fletum,** cry
      turgiduli: turgidulus-a-um, adj., swollen
      rubent: rubeo, rubere, rubui, be red, "bloodshot"

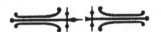

4

This poem is often read in conjunction with 31 and 46. The three seem informed by the same experience of journey. Here the poet empowers a vessel with speech. Friends *(hospites)* are invited to gaze upon an old ship, a *phaselus,* which has just carried its master, presumably Catullus, on a journey from Bithynia to Lake Garda, near his home at Sirmio. In reflecting on this recent journey, Catullus imaginatively sees the ship in its early stages as forest on the slopes of Mt. Cytorus near the city of Amastris, on the southern coast of the Black Sea. The catalog of place names traces the journey back to its starting place. The allegorical aspects of the poem must be considered. In what ways does the poet make the voyage of the ship reflect human experience? This meter, found only in Poems 4 and 29 of the Catullan corpus, is the iambic senarius (also called iambic trimeter), in which there are six iambs. Three meters or *metra* represent three groups of two iambs.

Phaselus ille, quem videtis, hospites,
ait fuisse navium celerrimus,
neque ullius natantis impetum trabis
nequisse praeterire, sive palmulis
opus foret volare sive linteo.   5
et hoc negat minacis Hadriatici
negare litus insulasve Cycladas
Rhodumque nobilem horridamque Thraciam
Propontida trucemve Ponticum sinum,
ubi iste post phaselus antea fuit   10
comata silva; nam Cytorio in iugo
loquente saepe sibilum edidit coma.
Amastri Pontica et Cytore buxifer,
tibi haec fuisse et esse cognitissima
ait phaselus: ultima ex origine   15
tuo stetisse dicit in cacumine,
tuo imbuisse palmulas in aequore,
et inde tot per impotentia freta
erum tulisse, laeva sive dextera
vocaret aura, sive utrumque Iuppiter   20
simul secundus incidisset in pedem;
neque ulla vota litoralibus deis
sibi esse facta, cum veniret a mari
novissimo hunc ad usque limpidum lacum.
sed haec prius fuere: nunc recondita   25
senet quiete seque dedicat tibi,
gemelle Castor et gemelle Castoris.

---

1 **phaselus: phaselus, -i,** m., ship (a Greek word); it denotes a bean-shaped craft of the type
   found in Egyptian tombs, perhaps suggestive of Charon's boat, the boat for passage across
   the Styx river after death.

2 **ait: aio,** (defective verb used mainly in present and imperfect) say
Celerrimus is in the nominative case although it is an adjective in indirect statement in Latin and should be in the accusative case; this Greek usage makes the subject of the infinitive **(fuisse)** in indirect statement the same case as the subject of the main verb **(ait)**; Catullus' imitation of this Greek construction is an example of a Hellenism. It might also be argued that since **phaselus** is Greek, if it could speak it would speak Greek.

3 **ullius: ullus-a-um,** adj., any
natantis: nato, natare, natavi, natatum, swim, float
trabis: trabs, -is, f., plank, beam

4 **nequisse: nequeo, nequire, nequii, nequitum,** be unable
praeterire: praetereo, praeterire, praeterii, praeteritum, pass by, surpass, go beyond
palmulis: palmula, -ae, f., little oar, oar blade

5 **opus foret: opus esse,** (idiom) there is need of
foret = esset
palmulis and **linteo:** both in the ablative case governed by **opus foret**
linteo: linteus, -i, m., sail, cloth

6 **hoc,** a demonstrative pronoun in the accusative case, neuter gender, object of the infinitive **negare,** referring to the speed boasted of in lines 1-5
minacis: minax, minacis, adj., threatening
Hadriatici: Hadriaticum, -i, n., Adriatic Sea, one of five place names (lines 6–9), subjects of the infinitive **negare** in an indirect statement introduced by **negat**

7 **Cycladas: Cyclades, Cycladum,** f., the Cyclades Islands; note the Grecism.

8 **Rhodum: Rhodus, -i,** f., island of Rhodes
Thraciam: Thracius-a-um, adj., of or belonging to Thrace

9 **Propontida** (Greek accusative): **Propontis, Propontidis,** f., the Propontis, the Sea of Marmora, separating the Black Sea from the Aegean; the Hellespont leads from the Aegean into the Sea of Marmora and the Bosphorus from the Sea of Marmora into the Black Sea, **Ponticum Sinum.**

10 Here **post,** the adverb meaning "afterwards," and **antea,** the adverb meaning "before," are used in sharp contrast like the stem and stern of the **phaselus** which they surround.

11 **comata: comatus-a-um,** adj., long-haired, leafy
Cytorio: Cytorius-a-um, adj., pertaining to Mount Cytorus on the south side of the Black Sea

12 **loquente: loquor, loqui, locutus sum,** speak
sibilum: sibilus, -i, m., hissing
edidit: edo, edere, edidi, editum, bring forth

13 **Amastri: Amastris, -is,** f., Amastris, a city near Mount Cytorus; this is the vocative form.
Cytore: Cytorus, -i, m., Mount Cytorus
buxifer: buxifer-buxifera-buxiferum, adj., producing boxwood trees

15 **ultima: ultimus-a-um,** adj., last, final, farthest. The phrase **ultima ex origine** conveys the notion of the English phrase "at birth."

16   cacumine: **cacumen, -inis,** n., extreme end of a thing, point, tip, peak

17   imbuisse: **imbuo, imbuere, imbui, imbutum,** wet, soak, saturate

18   impotentia: **impotens, impotentis,** adj., powerless to control, wild, furious, violent
     freta: **fretum, -i,** n., strait, sound, channel

19   erum: **erus, -i,** m., heir, master of the house (in respect to servants), owner

20   vocaret: subjunctive in indirect question as is **incidisset** in line 21
     aura: **aura, aurae,** f., breeze
     Iuppiter: metonymy for **ventus**

21   secundus: **secundus-a-um,** adj., favorable in the sense that the wind follows behind the ship
     incidisset: **incido, incidere, incidi, incasum,** fall upon, alight upon
     pedem: **pes, pedis,** m., foot; here, the foot of the sail

22   litoralibus: **litoralis-litorale,** adj., belonging to the shore

23   sibi, probably a dative of agent, found regularly in Greek with a perfect passive participle; so
       here with the perfect passive infinitive **facta esse,** a Grecism perhaps? **Sibi** is considered
       by some to be a dative of advantage, "on the ship's own behalf."

24   Here, **novissimo** may mean the last sea to be reached and not the farthest from this point.
       Thus it could be a reference to the Adriatic or to the Black Sea.
     limpidum: **limpidus-a-um,** adj., clear, bright, transparent
     lacum: **lacus, -us,** m., lake, pond

25   fuere = **fuerunt**
     recondita: **reconditus-a-um,** adj., hidden, concealed

26   senet: **seneo, senere, senui,** be old, age

27   Castor and Pollux were twin sons of Zeus who became protectors and patrons of sailors.

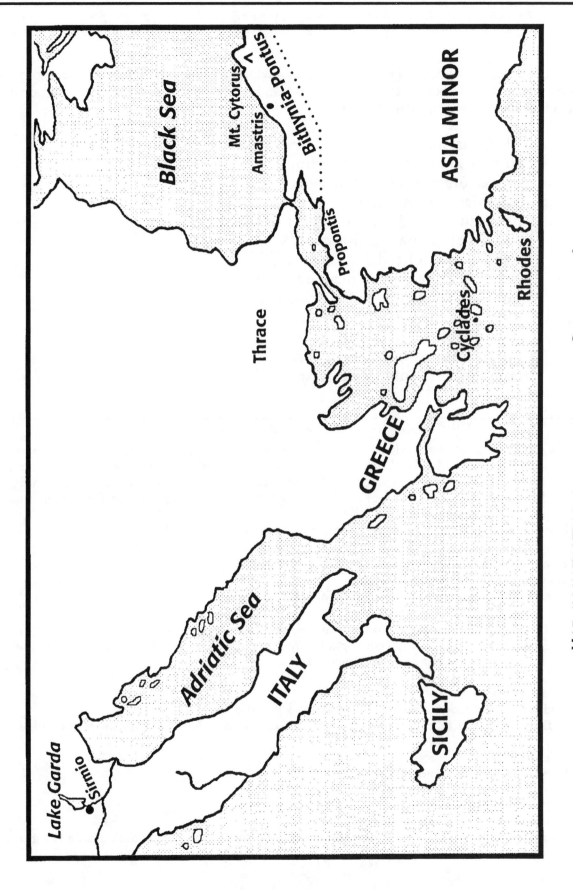

MAP ILLUSTRATING PLACES NAMED IN CATULLUS 4

5

This emotionally charged poem reflects the passion for which the poet is famous and seems to come from very intense, and probably very early, moments in his relationship with Clodia. The poem is written in the hendecasyllabic meter.

> Vivamus, mea Lesbia, atque amemus,
> rumoresque senum severiorum
> omnes unius aestimemus assis!
> soles occidere et redire possunt:
> nobis cum semel occidit brevis lux,　　　　　5
> nox est perpetua una dormienda.
> da mi basia mille, deinde centum,
> dein mille altera, dein secunda centum,
> deinde usque altera mille, deinde centum.
> dein, cum milia multa fecerimus,　　　　　10
> conturbabimus illa, ne sciamus,
> aut ne quis malus invidere possit,
> cum tantum sciat esse basiorum.

1　**vivamus: vivo, vivere, vixi, victum,** live. Lesbia is in the vocative case. In deriving this name from the island of Lesbos in the Aegean Sea, Catullus associates his girlfriend with the poet Sappho, who lived on this island. The name Lesbia may gloss the real name of his love, Clodia, the sister of Clodius, a rather sinister figure, and the focus of so much anxiety in the consulship of Cicero.
　　amemus: amo, amare, amavi, amatum, love, make love

2　**rumores: rumor, rumoris,** m., gossip, rumor
　　senum: senex, senis, m., old man
　　severiorum: severus-a-um, adj., strict, austere

3　**aestimemus: aestimo, aestimare, aestimavi, aestimatum,** evaluate, rate
　　assis: as, assis, m., a penny, a copper coin. **Assis** is in the genitive case, the genitive of price or value dependent upon **aestimemus.**

4　**soles: sol, solis,** m., sun
　　occidere: occido, occidere, occidi, occasum, set, fall down
　　redire: redeo, redire, redivi or **redii, reditum,** return, rise. Note the chiasmus in the line.

5　**semel: semel,** adv., once
　　brevis: brevis-breve, adj., brief, short
　　lux: lux, lucis, f., light

6　**nox: nox, noctis,** f., night, darkness
　　dormienda: dormio, dormire, dormivi or **dormii, dormitum,** sleep; **dormienda** is a gerundive.

7   **da: do, dare, dedi, datum,** give
     mi = mihi
     basia: basium, basii, n., kiss; **basium** appears for the first time in Roman literature in Catullus.
          Later authors such as Martial use the word frequently. Its origin is obscure; perhaps it
          was a dialectical word whose use was elevated by Catullus' poems; possibly it was na-
          tive to Catullus' home in northern Italy.
     deinde: deinde, adv., then

9   **usque:** adv., continuously, without a break

10   **fecerimus: facio, facere, feci, factum,** (future perfect form) make, do

11   **conturbabimus: conturbo, conturbare, conturbavi, conturbatum,** confuse, disturb, upset
     sciamus: scio, scire, scivi, scitum, know

12   **quis = aliquis:** (the indefinite pronoun) someone, anybody
     malus: malus-a-um, adj., bad, evil
     invidere: invideo, invidere, invidi, invisum, cast an evil eye upon

7

This poem reflects a time of great happiness in the relationship between Lesbia and Catullus; its tone and theme closely relate to Poem 5. The exotic place references in this poem belong to a poetic typology, perhaps originating in the Alexandrian poets. They lend an air of mystique and intrigue to what is already romantic. The poem is written in the hendecasyllabic meter.

Quaeris, quot mihi basiationes
tuae, Lesbia, sint satis superque.
quam magnus numerus Libyssae harenae
lasarpiciferis iacet Cyrenis
oraclum Iovis inter aestuosi   5
et Batti veteris sacrum sepulcrum;
aut quam sidera multa, cum tacet nox,
furtivos hominum vident amores:
tam te basia multa basiare
vesano satis et super Catullo est,   10
quae nec pernumerare curiosi
possint nec mala fascinare lingua.

---

1   **quaeris: quaero, quaerere, quaesivi, quaesitum**, seek, ask
     quot: quot, (interrogative adverb) how many
     basiationes: basiatio, basiationis, f., a kissing

2   **Tuae** modifies **basiationes** and probably is best taken as "your kissings (of me)."
     Sint is subjunctive in indirect question.
     satis superque: advs., enough and more than enough

3   **quam: quam**, adv., as
     Libyssae: Libyssus-a-um, adj., Libyan
     harenae: harena, harenae, f., sand, grain of sand

     silphium berry

4   **lasarpiciferis: lasarpicifer-lasarpicifera-lasarpiciferum**, adj., bearing or producing asafoe-
         tida; this plant was imported by Rome from Cyrene, and used for medicinal purposes,
         particularly during the time of Caesar. It was also represented on the official coinage of
         Cyrene.
     iacet: iaceo, iacere, iacui, iacitum, lie, recline
     Cyrenis: Cyrenae, Cyrenarum, f., Cyrene, the capital of Libya, was founded according to
         legend in the seventh century B.C. by Battus, who was later buried and worshipped at a
         shrine in the center of the city. In the third century B.C., Callimachus, a famous poet
         imitated by Catullus, was born in Cyrene. Callimachus claimed lineage from Battus, and
         Catullus refers to him as Battiades (65.16 and 116.2). This poem essentially alludes to
         Callimachus' poetry, which was well known in Catullus' time.

5   **oraclum: orac(u)lum, orac(u)li**, n., oracle; this may refer to the temple of Ammon, the Egyp-
         tian god equivalent to Zeus and Jupiter, known to have been the site of an oracle situated
         somewhere in the Libyan desert.
     aestuosi: aestuosus-a-um, adj., very hot, sultry

6 **veteris: vetus, veteris,** adj., old
 sacrum: sacer-sacra-sacrum, adj., sacred, holy, revered
 sepulcrum: sepulcrum, sepulcri, n., tomb, burial ground

7 **sidera: sidus, sideris,** n., star
 tacet: taceo, tacere, tacui, tacitum, be silent, still

8 **furtivos: furtivus-a-um,** adj., stolen, secret, hidden

9 **Te** is best taken as the direct object of the infinitive **basiare**, and **basia multa** would be adverbial accusatives with **basiare**. Note the chiasmus in the line.

10 **vesano: vesanus-a-um,** adj., not of sound mind, insane

11 **pernumerare: pernumero, pernumerare, pernumeravi, pernumeratum,** count up
 curiosi: curiosus-a-um, adj., inquisitive; its substantive meaning is "busybodies."

12 **fascinare: fascino, fascinare, fascinavi, fascinatum,** cast an evil eye upon, jinx, bewitch

8

The despair which pervades this poem suggests that its occasion must have been a catastrophic break-up between Lesbia and Catullus. Note the courage which the poet displays in composing the poem and balance that with the despair he exposes. The meter is limping iambics (choliambics or scazons).

> Miser Catulle, desinas ineptire,
> et quod vides perisse perditum ducas.
> fulsere quondam candidi tibi soles,
> cum ventitabas quo puella ducebat
> amata nobis quantum amabitur nulla.   5
> ibi illa multa cum iocosa fiebant,
> quae tu volebas nec puella nolebat,
> fulsere vere candidi tibi soles.
> nunc iam illa non volt: tu quoque
>   inpote<ns noli>,
> nec quae fugit sectare, nec miser vive,   10
> sed obstinata mente perfer, obdura.
> vale, puella. iam Catullus obdurat,
> nec te requiret nec rogabit invitam.
> at tu dolebis, cum rogaberis nulla.
> scelesta, vae te! quae tibi manet vita?   15
> quis nunc te adibit? cui videberis bella?
> quem nunc amabis? cuius esse diceris?
> quem basiabis? cui labella mordebis?
> at tu, Catulle, destinatus obdura.

---

1   desinas: desino, desinere, desii, desitum, cease, stop
     ineptire: ineptio, ineptire, make a fool of oneself

2   perisse: pereo, perire, perii, peritum, perish, die
     perditum: perdo, perdere, perdidi, perditum, destroy, ruin, lose
     Ducas is a jussive subjunctive from duco.

3   fulsere = fulserunt: fulgeo, fulgere, fulsi, shine
     candidi: candidus-a-um, adj., bright

4   ventitabas: ventito, ventitare, ventitavi, ventitatum, keep on going, keep following

5   Nobis is dative of agent with amata.

6   iocosa: iocosus-a-um, adj., joking, playful
     fiebant: fio, fieri, factus sum, happen, take place

7   Observe the litotes in this line.

9 **illa:** neuter plural or nominative singular? The impersonality of the third person nominative might lend a slight nuance to the rift between the lovers.
inpotens: inpotens, inpotentis, adj., uncontrolled, powerless
noli: nolo, nolle, nolui, not wish; the imperative followed by an infinitive means "don't."

10 **sectare: sector, sectari, sectatum,** run, chase, follow, run after; **sectare** is a form of the imperative.

11 **obstinata: obstinatus-a-um,** adj., resolute, determined, fixed
perfer: perfero, perferre, pertuli, perlatum, carry through, endure, put up with
obdura: obduro, obdurare, obduravi, obduratum, persist, stick it out

13 **requiret: requiro, requirere, requisivi, requisitum,** seek again, look after
invitam: invitus-a-um, adj., unwilling

15 **scelesta: scelestus-a-um,** wretched, unfortunate
vae: (interjection which governs the accusative or dative) alas, woe!

18 **labella: labellum, -i,** n., little lip
mordebis: mordeo, mordere, momordi, morsum, bite

19 **destinatus: destinatus-a-um,** adj., fixed, determined in mind

9

Friendship is one of the main values in the life and writings of Catullus. Veranius is addressed in later poems also and seems to have been a very intimate friend of Catullus. The counterpositioning of exuberance expressed in this poem with depression expressed in Poem 8 may be deliberate. The contrast in the tone of the two poems could not be more pronounced. The poem is written in the hendecasyllabic meter.

> Verani, omnibus e meis amicis
> antistans mihi milibus trecentis,
> venistine domum ad tuos penates
> fratresque unanimos anumque matrem?
> venisti. O mihi nuntii beati!　　　　　　　　5
> visam te incolumem audiamque Hiberum
> narrantem loca, facta, nationes,
> ut mos est tuus, applicansque collum
> iucundum os oculosque suaviabor.
> O quantum est hominum beatiorum,　　　　10
> quid me laetius est beatiusve?

2　antistans: antisto, antistare, antistiti, (with the dative case) surpass, excel

4　unanimos: unanimus-a-um, adj., of one mind, loving
anum: anus, anus, f., old woman (an adjective here)

5　nuntii beati: nominative case in exclamation

6　visam: viso, visere, visi, visum, see, behold
incolumem: incolumis-incolume, adj., unharmed, uninjured
Hiberum = Hiberorum: Hiber, Hiberis, m., an Iberian or Spaniard; Hiberi, -orum, m., the
　　　Iberians or Spaniards; Hiberus-a-um, adj., Iberian, Spanish

8　applicansque: applico, applicare, applicavi, applicatum, hold, embrace
collum: collum, -i, n., neck

9　iucundum: iucundus-a-um, adj., pleasing, pleasant
suaviabor: suavior, suaviari, suaviatus sum, kiss

MARBLE HEAD OF A YOUNG MAN FOUND IN THE 'HOUSE OF THE CITHARIST'
IN POMPEII. LINE DRAWING BY MALACHY EGAN.

10

This poem is occasioned by the accidental meeting of Catullus and his friend Varus in the Roman Forum. This Varus is probably Quintilius Varus, born in Cremona, who was known to Horace and Virgil. Quintilius Varus died in 24 B.C. and was the subject of a poem written by Horace and dedicated to Vergil (Odes I.24). The poem contains references to Catullus' return trip from Bithynia in late 57 or 56 B.C., where he had been with the governor Gaius Memmius. The poet injects dialogue into his poem; he behaves like a fool, and does not hesitate to communicate such an impression directly to the reader. Set between two very intense poems, this poem shows the sensitive and learned (*doctus*) poet at ease in less than poetic settings. The poem is written in hendecasyllabic meter.

Varus me meus ad suos amores
visum duxerat e foro otiosum,
scortillum, ut mihi tum repente visum est,
non sane illepidum neque invenustum.
huc ut venimus, incidere nobis   5
sermones varii, in quibus, quid esset
iam Bithynia, quo modo se haberet,
et quonam mihi profuisset aere.
respondi id quod erat, nihil neque ipsis
nec praetoribus esse nec cohorti,   10
cur quisquam caput unctius referret,
praesertim quibus esset irrumator
praetor, nec faceret pili cohortem.
'at certe tamen,' inquiunt 'quod illic
natum dicitur esse, comparasti   15
ad lecticam homines.' ego, ut puellae
unum me facerem beatiorem,
'non' inquam 'mihi tam fuit maligne,
ut, provincia quod mala incidisset,
non possem octo homines parare rectos.'   20
at mi nullus erat nec hic neque illic,
fractum qui veteris pedem grabati
in collo sibi collocare posset.
hic illa, ut decuit cinaediorem,
'quaeso,' inquit 'mihi, mi Catulle, paulum   25
istos commoda: nam volo ad Serapim
deferri.' 'mane,' inquii puellae,
'istud quod modo dixeram me habere,
fugit me ratio: meus sodalis—
Cinna est Gaius,—is sibi paravit.   30
verum, utrum illius an mei, quid ad me?
utor tam bene quam mihi pararim.
sed tu insulsa male et molesta vivis,
per quam non licet esse neglegentem.'

visum—syphe

2   **otiosum: otiosus-a-um,** adj., at leisure

3   **scortillum: scortum, -i,** n., prostitute, harlot; this is the diminutive form. Catullus' ongoing
       fondness for diminutive forms signals his affection or playfulness.
       repente, adv., suddenly, at that instant

4   **sane: sane,** adv., naturally, (with negatives) really, at all
       illepidum: illepidus-a-um, adj., inelegant
       invenustum: invenustus-a-um, adj., unattractive, homely. Note how the litotes of this line
       suggest the poet's unspoken interest in and tolerance of the **scortillum.**

5   **incidere = inciderunt: incido, incidere, incidi, incasum,** fall upon, happen

6   **sermones: sermo, sermonis,** m., conversation
       Esset is subjunctive in indirect question.

8   **quonam: quisnam-quaenam-quidnam,** (interrogative adjective) what, modifying **aere**
       aere: aes, aeris, n., bronze, (by metonymy) profit
       profuisset: prosum, prodesse, profui, benefit, be of profit to (with dative)

10   **praetoribus: praetor, praetoris,** m., governor
       cohorti: cohors, cohortis, m., the staff, retinue

11   **quisquam: quisquam-quaequam-quidquam,** (indefinite pronoun) anyone, someone
       unctius: unctus-a-um, adj., greasy, "slick." The reference is to becoming wealthier and more
       self-indulgent as a result of participation in the tour of duty in the province of Bithynia.

12   **praesertim: praesertim,** adv., particularly, especially
       quibus: the relative pronoun used as a dative of possession
       irrumator: irrumator, irrumatoris, m., a deviate, pervert; this is a very uncomplimentary
       reference to Gaius Memmius, the man who married Sulla's daughter Fausta and to whom
       Lucretius dedicated his great hexameter poem *De Rerum Natura* in 55 B.C.

13   **faceret pili: non facere pili,** an idiom meaning to care nothing about; **pilus, -i,** m., hair

14   **inquiunt: inquam,** (defective verb) say

15   **natum: nascor, nasci, natus sum,** be born, develop, transpire; the word seems to mean "the
       local product."
       comparasti = comparavisti: comparo, comparare, comparavi, comparatum, procure, obtain,
       purchase

16   **lecticam: lectica, -ae,** f., litter, essentially a couch which is to be carried like a man-moved taxi

17   **unum:** used here in the sense of "uniquely"
       beatiorem: beatus-a-um, adj., happy, lucky

18   **maligne: malignus-a-um,** adj., stingy, malicious

19   **incidisset: incido, incidere, incidi, incasum,** fall upon, come unexpectedly upon

20   **rectos: rectus-a-um,** adj., right, straight-backed; the word may refer to the youth and strength of the carriers; it may also play on the poetic context.

21   **mi = mihi:** dative of possession

22   **fractum: frango, frangere, fregi, fractum,** break
      pedem: pes, pedis, m., leg; here leg of a couch, cot
      grabati: grabatus, -i, m., a cot, a small couch

23   **collo: collum, -i,** n., neck
      collocare: colloco, collocare, collocavi, collocatum, place, put in order

24   **decuit: decet, decere, decuit,** it is becoming, it is suitable, it does seem proper
      cinaediorem: cinaedus-a-um, adj., shameless, crude

25   **quaeso: quaeso, quaesere, quaesivi, quaesitum,** seek, seek to obtain, "I beg" or "please"
      mi: vocative masculine singular of **meus-a-um,** adj., my. Notice the effect of repetition.
      paulum: paulum, adv., a little while

26   **commoda: commodo, commodare, commodavi, commodatum,** lend, give, bestow
      Serapim: Serapis, Serapis, m., the Egyptian god of healing, whose worship is first seen in Italy about the end of the second century B.C.; there were attempts to suppress the cult in 58 B.C.

27   **deferri: deferro, deferre, detuli, delatum,** bring down, carry down
      mane: maneo, manere, mansi, mansum, remain, wait

28   **modo: modo,** adv., just, now, only recently

29   **ratio: ratio, -ionis,** f., reason
      sodalis: sodalis, -is, m., comrade, companion

30   **Gaius Cinna:** a poet addressed in Poem 95, who had perhaps accompanied Catullus to Bithynia; notice the word order in this line.
      paravit = comparavit

31   **verum: verum,** adv., truly
      utrum: utrum, adv., whether

32   **utor: utor, uti, usus sum,** use
      pararim = paraverim = comparaverim

33 insulsa: **insulsus-a-um,** adj., tasteless, insipid
molesta: molestus-a-um, adj., troublesome, annoying
vivis: vivo, vivere, vixi, victum, live; here in the sense of "you are"

34 **licet: licet, licere, licuit,** it is permitted
neglegentem: neglegens, neglegentis, adj., careless, neglectful, relaxed

11

This poem is addressed to Catullus' friends Furius and Aurelius, and asks them to speak on Catullus' behalf to Lesbia. The biting message is motivated by the frustrated love of its speaker. The first sixteen lines constitute one sentence, a dramatic contrast to the taut impact of lines 17–20 and the touching final image in lines 21–24. The meter is Sapphic.

Furi et Aureli, comites Catulli,
sive in extremos penetrabit Indos,
litus ut longe resonante Eoa
    tunditur unda,
sive in Hyrcanos Arabasve molles,   5
seu Sagas sagittiferosve Parthos,
sive quae septemgeminus colorat
    aequora Nilus,
sive trans altas gradietur Alpes,
Caesaris visens monimenta magni,   10
Gallicum Rhenum, horribile aequor ulti-
    mosque Britannos,
omnia haec, quaecumque feret voluntas
caelitum, temptare simul parati,
pauca nuntiate meae puellae   15
    non bona dicta.
cum suis vivat valeatque moechis,
quos simul complexa tenet trecentos,
nullum amans vere, sed identidem omnium
    ilia rumpens;   20
nec meum respectet, ut ante, amorem,
qui illius culpa cecidit velut prati
ultimi flos, praetereunte postquam
    tactus aratro est.

---

2   **penetrabit: penetro, penetrare, penetravi, penetratum,** enter, get to, penetrate
Indos suggests the Roman Far East.

3   **litus: litus, litoris,** n., shore
ut: when followed by the indicative mood, it means "where" or "as."
resonante: resono, resonare, resonavi, resound, echo
Eoa: Eous-a-um, adj., eastern

4   **tunditur: tundo, tundere, tutudi, tunsum,** beat, pound, hammer

5   **Hyrcanos: Hyrcani, -orum,** m., people living on the shores of the Caspian Sea
Arabasve: Arabs, Arabis, adj. used as a substantive, an Arab
molles: mollis-molle, adj., soft, gentle

6 **Sagas: Sagae, -arum,** m., Scythians
sagittiferosve: sagittifer-sagittifera-sagittiferum, adj., arrow bearing
Parthos: Parthi, -orum, m., Parthians, people living in Parthia, a land northeast of Syria,
 bounded by the Tigris and Euphrates rivers

7 **septemgeminus: septemgeminus-a-um,** adj., sevenfold, here perhaps "seven-throated"

8 **Nilus: Nilus, -i,** m., Nile river

9 **gradietur: gradior, gradi, gressus sum,** go, journey

13 **omnia haec:** object of **temptare** in line 14
 quaecumque: quicumque-quaecumque-quodcumque, whatever
 voluntas: voluntas, voluntatis, f., wish, will

14 **caelitum: caeles, caelitis,** m./f., heaven-dweller, god

17 **vivat: vivo, vivere, vixi, victum,** live
 valeat: valeo, valere, valui, be strong, be healthy
 moechis: moechus, -i, m., adulterer

18 **complexa: complector, complecti, complexus sum,** embrace
 trecentos: trecenti-ae-a, adj., m., three hundred

19 **vere: vere,** adv., truly
 identidem: identidem, adv., continually, again and again

20 **ilia: ilia, ilium,** n. (plural), the groin
 rumpens: rumpo, rumpere, rupi, ruptum, break, burst

21 **respectet: respecto, respectare, respectavi, respectatum,** look back upon

22 **velut: velut,** adv., just as
 prati: pratum, -i, n., meadow

23 **ultimi: ultimus-a-um,** adj., ultimate, at the edge of
 flos: flos, floris, m., flower
 praetereunte: praetereo, praeterire, praeterivi, praeteritum, to go past
 beyond   pres persnple

24 **tactus: tango, tangere, tetigi, tactum,** touch
 aratro: aratrum, -i, n., plow

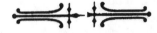

12

Addressed to Marrucinus Asinius, the brother of Gaius Asinius Pollio, builder of Rome's first library, this humorous poem uses a trivial situation to occasion a carefully veiled statement which affirms Catullus' fondness for what is really valuable. The gift of the napkin reminds Catullus of the true friendship behind that gift. That friendship is something precious. The meter is hendecasyllabic.

Marrucine Asini, manu sinistra
non belle uteris: in ioco atque vino
tollis lintea neglegentiorum.
hoc salsum esse putas? fugit te, inepte:
quamvis sordida res et invenusta est.   5
non credis mihi? crede Pollioni
fratri, qui tua furta vel talento
mutari velit: est enim leporum
differtus puer ac facetiarum.
quare aut hendecasyllabos trecentos   10
exspecta, aut mihi linteum remitte,
quod me non movet aestimatione,
verum est mnemosynum mei sodalis.
nam sudaria Saetaba ex Hiberis
miserunt mihi muneri Fabullus   15
et Veranius: haec amem necesse est
ut Veraniolum meum et Fabullum.

---

2   **belle: belle,** adv., neatly, nicely, well
    uteris: utor, uti, usus sum, use (with ablative)
    ioco: iocus, -i, m., jest, joke

3   **lintea: linteum, lintei,** n., linen cloth, napkin
    Neglegentiorum recalls Poem 10, line 34.

4   **salsum: salsus-a-um,** adj., salty, witty
    inepte: ineptus-a-um, adj., foolish

5   **quamvis: quamvis,** adv., however; the word intensifies the adjective which it modifies and
        has the sense of "as much as can be."
    sordida: sordidus-a-um, adj., in poor taste, crude
    invenusta: invenustus-a-um, adj., uncharming; the antithesis of anything tastefully done

7   **furta: furtum, -i,** n., theft
    talento: talentum, -i, n., a talent, a sum of money

8   **leporum: lepor, leporis,** m., pleasantness, charm, wit

9   **differtus: differtus-a-um,** adj., full of (with genitive)
    facetiarum: facetiae, -arum, f., clever things

11 **exspecta: exspecto, exspectare, exspectavi, exspectatum,** expect, wait for

12 **aestimatione: aestimatio, aestimationis,** f., esteem, value

13 **mnemosynum: mnemosynum, -i,** n., memento, reminder

14 **sudaria: sudarium, -ii,** n., a handkerchief, a napkin
   Saetaba: Saetabus-a-um, adj., Saetaban, belonging to Saetabis, a town in Spain
   Hiberis: Hiberi, -orum, m., the Spanish people; (by metonymy) Spain

15 **muneri: munus, muneris,** n., gift; used as a dative of purpose

16 **amem: amo, amare, amavi, amatum,** love; subjunctive with **necesse est**

ROMAN ORATOR,
FROM *COSTUMES OF THE GREEKS AND ROMANS* BY THOMAS HOPE.

13

Addressed to his friend Fabullus, who has perhaps just returned from travel in Spain, this poem presents the poet's mock-heroic invitation to dine with him. Such a theme was a standard poetic device found in Alexandrian poetry. Perhaps evoking such associations here, Catullus carefully repeats his invitation after making certain clear warnings. In contrast to the returning, well-heeled world traveler, the poet, as always, has a cobweb-filled wallet, so he says. The dining will satisfy only a mutual appetite for friendship, whetted by the intoxicating and erotic scent of perfume, a gift from Lesbia to Catullus, a reminder of the greatest love of his life. The chance to be together and to share is a kind of wealth, surely worth Fabullus' bringing the food, jokes, companions, the "stuff" of dinner. The poem is written in hendecasyllabic meter.

> Cenabis bene, mi Fabulle, apud me
> paucis, si tibi di favent, diebus,
> si tecum attuleris bonam atque magnam
> cenam, non sine candida puella
> et vino et sale et omnibus cachinnis.　　　　5
> haec si, inquam, attuleris, venuste noster,
> cenabis bene; nam tui Catulli
> plenus sacculus est aranearum.
> sed contra accipies meros amores
> seu quid suavius elegantiusve est:　　　　10
> nam unguentum dabo, quod meae puellae
> donarunt Veneres Cupidinesque,
> quod tu cum olfacies, deos rogabis,
> totum ut te faciant, Fabulle, nasum.

1　**cenabis: ceno, cenare, cenavi, cenatum,** dine

2　**paucis diebus:** within a few days; ablative of time within which
favent: faveo, favere, favi, fautum, favor, promote

3　**attuleris: affero, afferre, attuli, allatum,** bring, carry

5　**sale: sal, salis,** f., salt, (figurative) wit
cachinnis: cachinnus, -i, m., loud laughter

6/7　Note repetition of **attuleris** and **cenabis.**

8　**plenus: plenus-a-um,** adj., full
sacculus: sacculus, -i, m., little bag, purse, wallet, knapsack
aranearum: aranea, araneae, f., spider's web

9　**meros: merus-a-um,** adj., pure, unmixed; normally used of wine (see Poem 27, line 7)

10　**suavius: suavis-suave,** adj., pleasant, charming, agreeable
elegantiusve: elegans, elegantis, adj., elegant, charming, pleasing, rewarding

11   **unguentum: unguentum, -i,** n., ointment, perfume

12   **donarunt = donaverunt**

13   **olfacies: olfacio, olfacere, olfeci, olfactum,** to smell

14   **nasum: nasus, -i,** m., nose

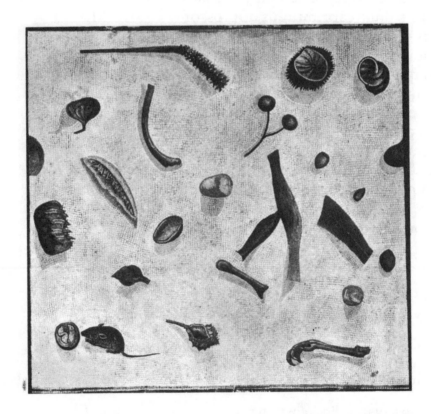

MOSAIC OF AN UNSWEPT FLOOR, FOUND ON THE AVENTINE IN ROME.

22

Suffenus is a bad poet according to Catullus because he is more concerned with the way the exterior of his works appears than with their contents. This is very different from the expectation which personal contact with Suffenus would arouse. In speech he is sharp-witted, intelligent and charming; in writing he is crude, unwitty and dull. But he has written a great deal and is only happy in the pursuit of writing. Catullus softens the sting of his critique by saying that it is easy to see the faults of others because they are in a sack in front of us and our own rest in a backpack whose position frustrates our view. The poem is written in limping iambics (choliambics or scazons).

Suffenus iste, Vare, quem probe nosti,
homo est venustus et dicax et urbanus,
idemque longe plurimos facit versus.
puto esse ego illi milia aut decem aut plura
perscripta, nec sic ut fit in palimpseston   5
relata: cartae regiae, novi libri,
novi umbilici, lora rubra membranae,
derecta plumbo et pumice omnia aequata.
haec cum legas tu, bellus ille et urbanus
Suffenus unus caprimulgus aut fossor   10
rursus videtur: tantum abhorret ac mutat.
hoc quid putemus esse? qui modo scurra
aut si quid hac re scitius videbatur,
idem infaceto est infacetior rure,
simul poemata attigit, neque idem umquam   15
aeque est beatus ac poema cum scribit:
tam gaudet in se tamque se ipse miratur.
nimirum idem omnes fallimur, neque est quisquam
quem non in aliqua re videre Suffenum
possis. suus cuique attributus est error;   20
sed non videmus manticae quod in tergo est.

---

1   **probe: probe,** adv., well, properly, correctly
      nosti = novisti: nosco, noscere, novi, notum, get to know

2   **venustus: venustus-a-um,** adj., beautiful, charming, attractive
      dicax: dicax, dicacis, adj., witty, sharp, sarcastic
      urbanus: urbanus-a-um, adj., of the city, of the town, sophisticated, "city slicker"

3   **versus: versus, -us,** m., line of writing

5   **fit: fio, fieri, factus sum,** prove to be, happen
      palimpseston (Greek accusative): **palimpsestum, -i,** n., an erased and reused manuscript

6   **relata: refero, referre, rettuli, relatum,** transfer, carry
      c(h)artae: charta, -ae, f., sheet of papyrus, paper

7   **umbilici: umbilicus, -i,** m., ornamental knobs at the end of the cylinder on which books
          were rolled
     lora: lorum, lori, n., strip of leather
     rubra: ruber-rubra-rubrum, adj., red, ruddy
     membranae: membrana, -ae, f., skin, parchment, possibly a sack or sleeve for the manuscript

8   **derecta = directa: dirigo, dirigere, direxi, directum,** make straight, level
     plumbo: plumbum, -i, n., lead, ruler for drawing lines so that each line of the manuscript
          would be perfectly parallel

9   **bellus: bellus-a-um,** adj., cute, fine, lovely

10   **caprimulgus: caprimulgus, -i,** m., a milker of goats
     fossor: fossor, fossoris, m., digger, lout, clown

11   **rursus: rursus,** adv., again, on the contrary
     abhorret: abhorreo, abhorrere, abhorrui, shrink back from, be inconsistent with, differ from

12   **scurra: scurra, -ae,** m., jester, comedian, man-about-town

13   **scitius: scitus-a-um,** adj., knowing, shrewd, witty

14   **infaceto: infacetus-a-um,** adj., dull, not witty
     rure: rus, ruris, n., the country, fields

15   **attigit: attingo, attingere, attigi, attactum,** touch, come into contact with, undertake

16   **aeque: aeque,** adv., equally

17   **gaudet: gaudeo, gaudere, gavisus sum,** rejoice at, find joy in

18   **nimirum: nimirum,** adv., without doubt, surely, clearly
     idem: idem (used as an adv.), in the same way, likewise
     fallimur: fallo, fallere, fefelli, falsum, to deceive, cheat

20   **attributus: attribuo, attribuere, attribui, attributum,** allot, bestow
     error: error, erroris, m., wandering, wavering, flaw

21   **manticae: mantica, -ae,** f., knapsack

27

This is a drinking song in hendecasyllabic meter.

> Minister vetuli puer Falerni,
> inger mi calices amariores,
> ut lex Postumiae iubet magistrae
> ebrioso acino ebriosioris.
> at vos quo lubet hinc abite, lymphae,   5
> vini pernicies, et ad severos
> migrate. hic merus est Thyonianus.

---

1   **minister: minister, ministri**, m., servant, attendant
     vetuli: vetulus-a-um, adj., old
     Falerni: Falernus-a-um, adj., Falernian, from a region in northern Campania noted for its
          wine

2   **inger: ingero, ingerere, ingessi, ingestum**, pour into; this form is an irregular singular im-
          perative.
     calices: calix, calicis, m., cup, pot
     amariores: amarus-a-um, adj., bitter

4   **ebrioso: ebriosus-a-um**, adj., drunken
     acino: acinus, -i, m., grape; the two elisions here and the polyptoton of **ebrioso** and **ebriosioris**
          are iconic in that they sound out the picture of excessive indulgence.

5   **lubet = libet, libere, libuit/libitum est**, it pleases
     lymphae: lympha, -ae, f., water

6   **pernicies: pernicies, -ei**, f., ruin
     severos: severus-a-um, adj., harsh, conservative; used substantively to mean perhaps "party-
          poopers"

7   **migrate: migro, migrare, migravi, migratum**, depart
     merus: merus-a-um, adj., pure, unmixed, i.e., not mixed with water
     Thyonianus: Thyonianus, -i, m., son of Thyone, i.e., Bacchus

31

This poem expresses the poet's joy upon return to his native Sirmio after the celebrated trip to Bithynia completed in 56 B.C. The poem lends itself to associations with Poems 4 and 46. The meter is limping iambics (choliambics or scazons).

Paene insularum, Sirmio, insularumque
ocelle, quascumque in liquentibus stagnis
marique vasto fert uterque Neptunus,
quam te libenter quamque laetus inviso,
vix mi ipse credens Thuniam atque Bithunos   5
liquisse campos et videre te in tuto.
O quid solutis est beatius curis,
cum mens onus reponit, ac peregrino
labore fessi venimus larem ad nostrum,
desideratoque acquiescimus lecto?   10
hoc est quod unum est pro laboribus tantis.
salve, O venusta Sirmio, atque ero gaude
gaudente, vosque, O Lydiae lacus undae,
ridete quidquid est domi cachinnorum.

---

2 **ocelle: ocellus, -i,** m., eye, here "jewel"
   liquens, liquentis, adj., liquid, fluid, clear
   stagnis: stagnum, -i, n., standing or still water

6 **liquisse: linquo, linquere, liqui,** leave, abandon

7 **solutis: solvo, solvere, solvi, solutum,** release, set free

8 **peregrino: peregrinus-a-um,** adj., foreign

9 **larem: lar, laris,** m., household god, (by metonymy) hearth, dwelling, home

10 **acquiescimus: acquiesco, acquiescere, acquievi, acquietum,** become physically quiet, re-
      pose, rest
   lecto: lectus, -i, m., bed

12 **ero: erus, -i,** m., master of the house (in respect to servants), owner

13 **Lydiae: Lydius-a-um,** adj., Lydian, Etruscan
   lacus: lacus, -us, m., lake, pond

14 **cachinnorum: cachinnus, -i,** m., loud laugh, a jeering; used by some authors to suggest the
      noise of clashing waves

34

This formulaic hymn to Diana features six quatrains, performed by a chorus of boys and girls. Perhaps an imitation of a Greek prototype, the poem uses a meter in which the first three lines of each quatrain are glyconics and last line is a pherecratean.

compulsory poem

Dianae sumus in fide
puellae et pueri integri:
<Dianam pueri integri>
puellaeque canamus.

O Latonia, maximi   5
magna progenies Iovis,
quam mater prope Deliam
deposivit olivam,

montium domina ut fores
silvarumque virentium   10
saltuumque reconditorum
amniumque sonantum:

tu Lucina dolentibus
Iuno dicta puerperis,
tu potens Trivia et notho es   15
dicta lumine Luna.

anastrophe

tu cursu, dea, menstruo
metiens iter annuum,
rustica agricolae bonis
tecta frugibus exples.   20

sis quocumque tibi placet
sancta nomine, Romulique,
antique ut solita es, bona
sospites ope gentem.

homage

request

---

2 **integri: integer, integra, integrum,** adj., chaste

5 **Latonia:** daughter of Latona (Leto), i.e., Diana (Artemis)

6 **progenies: progenies, progeniei,** f., offspring

7 **Deliam: Delius-a-um**, adj., relating to Delos, the island where Apollo and Artemis were born to Leto, who had been impregnated by Zeus

8   **olivam: oliva, -ae**, f., olive; the tree allegedly witnessed the birth of Apollo and Artemis.

9   **fores = esses**

11   **saltuumque: saltus, saltus**, m., forest
      reconditorum: reconditus-a-um, adj., hidden

12   **amniumque: amnis, amnis**, m./f., river
      sonantum = sonantium: sono, sonare, sonui, sonitum, sound

13   **Lucina** is the goddess of childbirth. The word is an epithet which associates the childbirth
      function of Diana (Artemis) with Juno.
      dolentibus: doleo, dolere, dolui, dolitum, grieve

14   **puerperis: puerpera, -ae**, f., a woman in childbirth; dative of agent with the perfect participle
      passive, **dicta**

15   **Trivia = Diana**: the word is a conflation of **tres** and **viae**, "three roads," and denotes the
      intersections where small shrines were frequently dedicated to Hecate, Diana's alter ego,
      associating her with the underworld.
      notho: nothus-a-um, adj., not genuine, false, phoney, "pale"

16   **Luna**: Diana's name when she is associated with the moon

17   **menstruo: menstruus-a-um**, adj., monthly

18   **metiens: metior, metiri, mensus sum**, measure, travel

19   **rustica: rusticus-a-um**, adj., rural, rustic

20   **frugibus: frux, frugis**, f., fruit, produce
      exples: expleo, explere, explevi, expletum, fill

23   **antique: antique**, adv., in ancient times
      solita es: soleo, solere, solitus sum, be accustomed

24   **sospites: sospito, sospitare, sospitavi, sospitatum**, preserve, protect
      ope: ops, opis, f., power, help

35

This hendecasyllabic poem invites Caecilius, an otherwise unknown writer-friend of Catullus, to leave his home town of Como in northern Italy and visit Catullus in Verona. The poem becomes a metrical letter; it is one of the few pieces which can be dated, since the settlement of New Como was established by Julius Caesar in 59 B.C.

Poetae tenero, meo sodali,
velim Caecilio, papyre, dicas
Veronam veniat, Novi relinquens
Comi moenia Lariumque litus.
nam quasdam volo cogitationes   5
amici accipiat sui meique.
quare, si sapiet, viam vorabit,
quamvis candida milies puella
euntem revocet, manusque collo
ambas iniciens roget morari.   10
quae nunc, si mihi vera nuntiantur,
illum deperit impotente amore.
nam quo tempore legit incohatam
Dindymi dominam, ex eo misellae
ignes interiorem edunt medullam.   15
ignosco tibi, Sapphica puella
musa doctior; est enim venuste
Magna Caecilio incohata Mater.

---

1 **tenero: tener-tenera-tenerum,** adj., gentle

2 **velim:** present subjunctive from **volo, velle, volui,** wish, want
 papyre: papyrus, -i, m./f., papyrus

4 **Lariumque: Larius-a-um,** adj., of or belonging to Lake Como

5 **cogitationes: cogitatio, cogitationis,** f., reflection

7 **sapiet: sapio, sapere, sapivi,** have a sense of, have a taste of, have knowledge of, be wise
 vorabit: voro, vorare, voravi, voratum, swallow, devour

8 **quamvis: quamvis,** conj., although
 milies: milies, adv., a thousand, innumerable times
 euntem: (pres act participle) going

10 **ambas: ambo-ae-o,** adj., both
 iniciens: inicio, inicere, inieci, iniectum, throw on, cast on
 morari: moror, morari, moratus sum, delay

12   **deperit: depereo, deperire, deperii**, be desperately in love with
      impotente: impotens, impotentis, adj., uncontrollable

13   **legit: lego, legere, legi, lectum**, read
      incohatam: incohatus-a-um, adj., begun (not finished)

14   **Dindymi dominam:** Dindymus is a mountain in Phrygia and was the center of worship for
          the mother goddess Cybele.
      misellae: misellus-a-um, adj., poor little

15   **edunt: edo, edere, edi, esum**, consume
      medullam: medulla, -ae, f., marrow

16   **ignosco: ignosco, ignoscere, ignovi, ignotum**, pardon, forgive, excuse, have sympathy for
      Sapphica: Sapphicus-a-um, adj., of or belonging to Sappho, the great lyric poet from the
          island of Lesbos

17   **doctior: doctus-a-um**, adj., learned
      venuste: venuste, adv., charmingly

18   **incohata: incoho, incohare, incohavi, incohatum**, begin
      Caecilio: dative of agent
      Magna Mater is the title of Caecilius' new poem.
      Cybele - E. goddess; goddess of earth, fertility, grain, propitiousness

36

This poem conveys the impression that Lesbia has made a vow to Venus and Cupid that if Catullus would return to her and would end his sarcastic writing, she would offer up in sacrifice the best poems of the worst poet. The implication is that to Lesbia this meant that she would sacrifice selected verses of Catullus. But to Catullus, this means the poetry of that most awful poet Volusius. The meter is hendecasyllabic.

Annales Volusi, cacata carta,
votum solvite pro mea puella.
nam sanctae Veneri Cupidinique
vovit, si sibi restitutus essem
desissemque truces vibrare iambos,   5
electissima pessimi poetae
scripta tardipedi deo daturam
infelicibus ustulanda lignis.
et hoc pessima se puella vidit
iocose lepide vovere divis.   10
nunc o caeruleo creata ponto,
quae sanctum Idalium Uriosque apertos
quaeque Ancona Cnidumque harundinosam
colis quaeque Amathunta quaeque Golgos
quaeque Durrachium Hadriae tabernam,   15
acceptum face redditumque votum,
si non illepidum neque invenustum est.
at vos interea venite in ignem,
pleni ruris et inficetiarum
annales Volusi, cacata carta.   20

---

1   Annales: annalis, -is, m., yearly record, annal
    cacata: caco, cacare, cacavi, cacatum, defile, defecate
    carta: carta, -ae, f., paper

2   solvite: solvo, solvere, solvi, solutum, dissolve, break up, free, release
    votum: votum, -i, n., solemn vow

4   vovit: voveo, vovere, vovi, votum, vow
    restitutus: restituo, restituere, restitui, restitutum, restore

5   desissemque: desino, desinere, desii, desitum, give up, abandon, stop from
    truces: trux, trucis, adj., savage, grim, fierce
    vibrare: vibro, vibrare, vibravi, vibratum, brandish, shake, flick

6   electissima: electus-a-um, adj., select, picked

7   tardipedi: tardipes, tardipedis, adj., slow-footed, limping

8   infelicibus: infelix, infelicis, adj., unlucky
    ustulanda: ustulo, ustulare, ustulavi, ustulatum, burn a little, scorch
    lignis: lignum, -i, n., wood, firewood

9   **Pessima** must be nominative case to fit the meter.

10 iocose: iocose, adv., humorously
    lepide: lepide, adv., charmingly

11 caeruleo: caeruleus-a-um, adj., blue
    creata: creo, creare, creavi, creatum, create, beget

12 **Idalium** was a city on Cyprus, center for the worship of Venus.
    Uriosque: Urii may refer to Uria, a city in the southern part of Apulia between Brundisium
        and Tarentum.

13 **Ancona** was a town near Picenum, modern Osculi Piceno, on Italy's Adriatic coast. Cnidus
        was the famed point on the southwest coast of Asia Minor where Praxiteles' great statue
        of Aphrodite was displayed.
    harundinosam: harundinosus-a-um, adj., overgrown with reeds

14 **Amathunta . . . Golgos:** Amathus and Golgi were two towns located on Cyprus.

15 **Durrachium** was the landing port in Illyria for ships which departed from Brundisium, and
        hence was a very heavily used seaport.

16 **face:** imperative form of **facio** (here instead of the more usual **fac**).

19 pleni: plenus-a-um, adj., full of (with genitive)
    inficetiarum: inficetiae, -arum, f., coarse jokes

43

This hendecasyllabic poem expresses shock and dismay at any attempt to compare the matchless Lesbia with anybody, particularly the addressed though unnamed girlfriend of the man from Formio, Mamurra.

> Salve, nec minimo puella naso
> nec bello pede nec nigris ocellis
> nec longis digitis nec ore sicco
> nec sane nimis elegante lingua,
> decoctoris amica Formiani.   5
> ten provincia narrat esse bellam?
> tecum Lesbia nostra comparatur?
> O saeclum insapiens et infacetum!

---

1 **Salve: salveo, salvere, salui**, be healthy; the imperative form means "hail" or "hello."
naso: nasus, -i, m., nose

2 **bello: bellus-a-um**, adj., pretty, attractive
ocellis – diminutive

3 **digitis: digitus, -i**, m., finger
ore: os, oris, n., mouth
sicco: siccus-a-um, adj., dry

4 **sane: sane**, adv., really, fully
nec nimis: nec nimis, adv., not particularly

5 **decoctoris: decoctor, decoctoris**, m., bankrupt

6 *ten – syncope for tenete*

7 While apparently using the "royal we," Catullus may imply by his use of **nostra** that Lesbia, because she is so wonderfully beautiful, belongs to all those who appreciate beauty.

8 **saeclum: saeculum, -i**, n., age
infacetum: infacetus-a-um, adj., dull

cf Cicero "In Cat I"
O time! O customs!
(O tempora! O mores!)

colloquialisms
ten – tene
tun – tune
ain – aitne (aisne)
satin – satisne
viden – videsne

WALL PAINTING OF A GIRL POURING PERFUME, FROM 'THE FARNESINA,'
A LUXURIOUS ROMAN HOUSE ALONG THE TIBER.
LINE DRAWING BY MALACHY EGAN.

44

Sestius, a friend of Catullus, has invited the poet to dinner. However, before he goes, Catullus must read a speech recently written by Sestius. The speech is so chilling from a literary point of view that Catullus contracts a cold and must return to his safe, sound but simple abode where he can recover. Like Poems 8, 22, and 31, the meter is limping iambic (choliambic or scazon).

O funde noster seu Sabine seu Tiburs
(nam te esse Tiburtem autumant, quibus non est
cordi Catullum laedere; at quibus cordi est,
quovis Sabinum pignore esse contendunt),
sed seu Sabine sive verius Tiburs,   5
fui libenter in tua suburbana
villa, malamque pectore expuli tussim,
non immerenti quam mihi meus venter,
dum sumptuosas appeto, dedit, cenas.
nam, Sestianus dum volo esse conviva,   10
orationem in Antium petitorem
plenam veneni et pestilentiae legi.
hic me gravedo frigida et frequens tussis
quassavit usque, dum in tuum sinum fugi,
et me recuravi otioque et urtica.   15
quare refectus maximas tibi grates
ago, meum quod non es ulta peccatum.
nec deprecor iam, si nefaria scripta
Sesti recepso, quin gravedinem et tussim
non mi, sed ipsi Sestio ferat frigus,   20
qui tunc vocat me, cum malum librum legi.

---

1   **funde: fundus, -i,** m., a piece of land, a farm, an estate
    Sabine: Sabinus-a-um, adj., Sabine, of or belonging to the Sabines, a people who neighbored the Latins and who eventually merged with the original settlers of Romulus' Rome; Catullus intends to contrast a rustic and unpretentious villa with its opposite, namely a sophisticated and aristocratic villa.
    Tiburs: Tiburs, Tiburtis, adj., of or belonging to Tibur (Tivoli), a town on the Anio river, northeast of Rome, considered a fashionable and aristocratic location for one's country estate or villa

2   **autumant: autumo, autumare, autumavi, autumatum,** affirm, assert

3   **laedere: laedo, laedere, laesi, laesum,** to knock, hurt, strike

4   **quovis: quivis-quaevis-quodvis,** (indefinite adjective) any, any you please, any at all
    pignore: pignus, pignoris, n., pledge, token
    quovis pignore contendere: (an idiom) to bet anything

5 verius: **verus-a-um,** adj., true, real

6 fui libenter: idiomatic for "I was delighted"
suburbana: **suburbanus-a-um,** adj., situated near Rome

7 expuli: **expello, expellere, expuli, expulsum,** drive out, drive away, eject
tussim: **tussis, tussis,** f., cough

8 immerenti: **immerens, immerentis,** adj., undeserving
venter: **venter, ventris,** m., stomach (metonymy for greed or appetite)

9 sumptuosas: **sumptuosus-a-um,** adj., very expensive, costly, lavish, extravagant
appeto: **appeto, appetere, appetivi, appetitum,** strive after, try to get, grasp after, have an
appetite for

10 conviva: **conviva, -ae,** m., guest, table companion

11 petitorem: **petitor, petitoris,** m., candidate

12 plenam: **plenus-a-um,** adj., full of (with genitive case)
veneni: **venenum, -i,** n., poison
pestilentiae: **pestilentia, -ae,** f., plague, sickness, unwholesome atmosphere
legi: **lego, legere, legi, lectum,** read, pick, traverse

13 gravedo: **gravedo, gravedinis,** f., cold, head cold

14 quassavit: **quasso, quassare, quassavi, quassatum,** keep shaking or tossing
sinum: **sinus, -us,** m., bay, curve, fold, lap
fugi: **fugio, fugere, fugi, fugitum,** flee

15 recuravi: **recuro, recurare, recuravi, recuratum,** restore, refresh, restore to health
urtica: **urtica, -ae,** f., nettle (an herb); notice how this line uses two fundamentally different
things, **otio** and **urtica,** instrumentally with the same verb; this figure of speech is zeugma.

16 refectus: **refectus-a-um,** adj., refreshed

17 ulta: **ulciscor, ulcisci, ultus sum,** avenge oneself on, punish
peccatum: **peccatum, -i,** n., slip, fault, mistake

18 deprecor: **deprecor, deprecari, deprecatus sum,** pray against
nefaria: **nefarius-a-um,** adj., impious, abominable

19 recepso: **recipio, recipere, recepi, receptum,** welcome into one's house; this form is an ar-
chaic future perfect.
quin: conjunction regularly used in a clause of doubt, introduced here by **deprecor**

45

This carefully constructed poem presents paired dialogue between a Greek woman, Acme, and her Roman lover, Septimius. From the opening contraposition of their names, the poem uses doublets and pairings throughout. The couple's artificial and hyperbolic responses create an exchange, which the reader/listener is asked to evaluate by the final rhetorical question, "Has anybody ever seen a more auspicious love?" The reader/listener is tempted to say, "Of course, we have! It's you and Lesbia." The meter is hendecasyllabic.

Acmen Septimius suos amores
tenens in gremio 'mea' inquit 'Acme,
ni te perdite amo atque amare porro
omnes sum assidue paratus annos,
quantum qui pote plurimum perire,   5
solus in Libya Indiaque tosta
caesio veniam obvius leoni.'
hoc ut dixit, Amor sinistra ut ante
dextra sternuit approbationem.
at Acme leviter caput reflectens   10
et dulcis pueri ebrios ocellos
illo purpureo ore suaviata,
'sic,' inquit 'mea vita Septimille,
huic uni domino usque serviamus,
ut multo mihi maior acriorque   15
ignis mollibus ardet in medullis.'
hoc ut dixit, Amor sinistra ut ante
dextra sternuit approbationem.
nunc ab auspicio bono profecti
mutuis animis amant amantur.   20
unam Septimius misellus Acmen
mavult quam Syrias Britanniasque:
uno in Septimio fidelis Acme
facit delicias libidinesque.
quis ullos homines beatiores   25
vidit, quis Venerem auspicatiorem?

---

1   **Acmen: Acme, -es,** f., Acme, the name of a Greek woman; this is a Greek accusative form.
    Septimius: name of Acme's lover

2   **gremio: gremium, -ii,** n., lap

3   **perdite: perdite,** adv., recklessly
    porro: porro, adv., further, on and on

4   **assidue: assidue,** adv., continually

5 **pote = potest**
perire: pereo, perire, perii, peritum, be desperately in love

6 **tosta: torreo, torrere, torrui, tostum,** roast, bake, burn

7 **caesio: caesius-a-um,** gray-eyed, blue-eyed
obvius: obvius-a-um, adj., meeting with (with dative)

8 **Amor** is Cupid.

9 **sternuit: sternuo, sternuere, sternui,** sneeze, sputter
approbationem: approbatio, approbationis, f., approval

10 **leviter: leviter,** adv., lightly, a little
reflectens: reflecto, reflectere, reflexi, reflexum, bend back, turn back

11 **ebrios: ebrius-a-um,** adj., drunken

12 **purpureo: purpureus-a-um,** adj., deep red
ore: os, oris, n., mouth
suaviata: suavior, suaviari, suaviatus sum, kiss

13 **Septimille** is the diminutive, vocative form of Septimius.

14 **usque: usque,** adv., continually
serviamus: servio, servire, servivi, be a servant or slave to

16 **mollibus: mollis-molle,** adj., soft, gentle
medullis: medulla, -ae, f., marrow

19 **auspicio: auspicium, -ii,** n., augury, the study of the flight of birds; for Romans the left side
was the **pars familiaris.** Acme sits in Septimius' lap and thus her right side meets with
Septimius' left side. Perhaps Cupid sneezes on both sides to seal the good fortune of
each no matter what position they are in. This might explain the use of **auspicio,** a direct
reference to the process of such determinings.
profecti: proficiscor, proficisci, profectus sum, set out, advance, walk away

20 **amant amantur:** example of polyptoton and asyndeton

21 The chiasmus in this line gives the impression that Acme has Septimius wrapped up.

22 The references to **Syrias Britanniasque** may suggest the year 55 B.C., when expeditions by
Crassus and Caesar were being discussed.

23 Uno recalls **unam** of line 21.

24 **delicias libidinesque:** hendiadys
libidinesque: libido, libidinis, f., longing, fancy, inclination

26 **Venerem:** the goddess Venus, (by metonymy) love
auspicatiorem: auspicatus-a-um, adj., well-omened

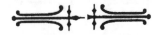

46

Most probably this poem celebrates Catullus' personal anticipation in the spring of 56 B.C. of departure from Bithynia for home via famed places along the return route. The meter is hendecasyllabic.

Iam ver egelidos refert tepores,
iam caeli furor aequinoctialis
iucundis Zephyri silescit aureis.
linquantur Phrygii, Catulle, campi
Nicaeaeque ager uber aestuosae: 5
ad claras Asiae volemus urbes.
iam mens praetrepidans avet vagari,
iam laeti studio pedes vigescunt.
O dulces comitum valete coetus,
longe quos simul a domo profectos   10
diversae varie viae reportant.

---

1   **ver: ver, veris,** n., spring-time
    egelidos: egelidus-a-um, adj., chilly, chill, mild
    tepores: tepor, teporis, m., gentle warmth, lukewarmness

2   **aequinoctialis: aequinoctialis-aequinoctiale,** adj., time of equal day and night, equinoctial

3   **iucundis: iucundus-a-um,** adj., pleasant, agreeable
    Zephyri: Zephyrus, -i, m., west wind
    silescit: silesco, silescere, be silent, grow quiet
    aureis: aura, -ae, f., wind, breeze; **aureis = auris**

4   **Phrygii campi = Bithyni campi** (Poem 31, line 5)

5   **Nicaeaeque: Nicaea, -ae,** f., Nicaea, capital city of Bithynia
    uber: uber, uberis, adj., fruitful
    aestuosae: aestuosus-a-um, adj., billowy, sultry

7   **praetrepidans: praetrepidans, praetrepidantis,** adj., excited, eager, very nervous, trembling
        with anticipation
    avet: aveo, avere, wish, want, desire strongly
    vagari: vagor, vagari, vagatus sum, wander

8   **vigescunt: vigesco, vigescere, vigui,** gain strength, become lively, become vigorous

9   **coetus: coetus, -us,** m., meeting, crowd

11 **varie: varie,** adv., differently

49

This puzzling hendecasyllabic poem, addressed to Cicero, can be either sarcastic or flattering. Could the poet be grateful to Cicero for omitting reference to his name in the *Pro Caelio*, a speech delivered in 56 B.C., which defamed Clodia (Lesbia) at one point? But, how could Catullus praise the one orator who destroyed his lover's reputation? Since the poet holds himself and his work in high esteem, by as much as he is the "worst" of poets, so is Cicero the "best" lawyer *(patronus)*, a subtle denunciation of the orator by the poet.

> Disertissime Romuli nepotum,
> quot sunt quotque fuere, Marce Tulli,
> quotque post aliis erunt in annis,
> gratias tibi maximas Catullus
> agit pessimus omnium poeta,　　　　　　　　5
> tanto pessimus omnium poeta,
> quanto tu optimus omnium patronus.

1　**disertissime: disertus-a-um**, adj., articulate, eloquent
　nepotum: nepos, nepotis, m., descendant, grandchild

2　**fuere = fuerunt**

6/7　**tanto ... quanto:** by as much as ... so much

BUST OF CICERO,
SECOND CENTURY A.D.

50

Licinius Calvus, friend of Catullus, was an orator and poet. Here Catullus and his friend exchanged witty barbs to such an extent that Catullus is apparently moved very much by his talented friend. The mock serious tone of this hendecasyllabic poem presages a second appearance of Calvus in Poem 53.

Hesterno, Licini, die otiosi
multum lusimus in meis tabellis,
ut convenerat esse delicatos:
scribens versiculos uterque nostrum
ludebat numero modo hoc modo illoc,   5
reddens mutua per iocum atque vinum.
atque illinc abii tuo lepore
incensus, Licini, facetiisque,
ut nec me miserum cibus iuvaret
nec somnus tegeret quiete ocellos,   10
sed toto indomitus furore lecto
versarer, cupiens videre lucem,
ut tecum loquerer simulque ut essem.
at defessa labore membra postquam
semimortua lectulo iacebant,   15
hoc, iucunde, tibi poema feci,
ex quo perspiceres meum dolorem.
nunc audax cave sis, precesque nostras,
oramus, cave despuas, ocelle,
ne poenas Nemesis reposcat a te.   20
est vemens dea: laedere hanc caveto.

---

1   hesterno: **hesternus-a-um**, adj., yesterday
     otiosi: **otiosus-a-um**, adj., at leisure, relaxing

2   lusimus: **ludo, ludere, lusi, lusum,** play
     tabellis: **tabella, -ae,** f., board, writing tablet

3   convenerat: **convenio, convenire, conveni, conventum,** be fitting or proper; (impersonal usage) it is agreed
     delicatos: **delicatus-a-um,** adj., cute, fancy, racy

4   versiculos: **versiculus, -i,** m., small verse, bits of verse
     uterque: **uterque-utraque-utrumque,** (indefinite adjective/pronoun) each one of two, both
     nostrum: of us (genitive plural of the first personal pronoun)

5   ludebat: **ludo, ludere, lusi, lusum,** play
     numero: **numerus, -i,** m., meter
     modo: **modo,** adv., just, now, only recently

6 **reddens: reddo, reddere, reddidi, redditum,** return, give back
 mutua: mutuus-a-um, adj., mutual; understood is **dicta.**

7 **illinc: illinc,** adv., from there
 lepore: lepor, -oris, m., pleasantness, charm, wit

8 **incensus: incensus-a-um,** adj., inflamed, burned up, set on fire
 facetiisque: facetiae, -arum, f., clever talk, humor

10 **tegeret: tego, tegere, texi, tectum,** cover, protect

11 **indomitus: indomitus-a-um,** adj., untamed, wild

12 **versarer: verso, versare, versavi, versatum,** turn

15 **lectulo: lectulus, -i,** m., small couch, cot

16 **iucunde: iucundus-a-um,** adj., pleasing, delightful
 poema: poema, poematis, n., poem (a Greek noun)

19 **despuas: despuo, despuere, despui, desputum,** spit upon, show contempt for

20 **Nemesis** is the goddess of vengeance.

21 **vemens = vehemens: vehemens, vehementis,** adj., violent, impetuous, vehement
 laedere: laedo, laedere, laesi, laesum, offend, hurt
 caveto: second person singular future imperative

51

Using a poem by Sappho as a model, Catullus has translated the original Greek into Latin but has also liberally used figures of speech throughout his version. The poem is inspired by the poet's sense of awe upon seeing, even imagining, the stunning and spellbinding presence of his beautiful Lesbia. The meter is Sapphic as in Poem 11.

> Ille mi par esse deo videtur,
> ille, si fas est, superare divos,
> qui sedens adversus identidem te
>   spectat et audit
>
> dulce ridentem, misero quod omnis   5
> eripit sensus mihi: nam simul te,
> Lesbia, aspexi, nihil est super mi
>   * * * * * * * * * * * *
>
> lingua sed torpet, tenuis sub artus
> flamma demanat, sonitu suopte   10
> tintinant aures, gemina teguntur
>   lumina nocte.
>
> otium, Catulle, tibi molestum est:
> otio exsultas nimiumque gestis:
> otium et reges prius et beatas   15
>   perdidit urbes.

---

3   **adversus: adversus-a-um,** adj., opposite, facing
     identidem: identidem, adv., again and again, constantly

5   **dulce: dulce,** adv., sweetly
     ridentem: rideo, ridere, risi, risum, smile

6   **mihi:** dative of separation
     nam simul: for as soon as

7   **aspexi: aspicio, aspicere, aspexi, aspectum,** catch sight of, spot, look closely at, observe

9   **torpet: torpeo, torpere, torpui,** be numb, be stiff
     tenuis: tenuis-tenue, adj., tender

10   **demanat: demano, demanare, demanavi,** flow down
     sonitu: sonitus, -us, m., sound
     suopte: suopte, adj., form of **suus = suo + pte;** an emphatic ablative

11   **tintinant: tintino, tintinare, tintinavi,** ring, tingle

aures: **auris, auris,** f., ear
gemina: **geminus-a-um,** adj., twin, both; this adjective is in the ablative case.
teguntur: **tego, tegere, texi, tectum,** cover, cloak

13 otium: **otium, otii,** n., free time, ease, leisure
molestum: **molestus-a-um,** adj., troublesome, irksome

14 exsultas: **exsulto, exsultare, exsultavi, exsultatum,** revel in, boast about
gestis: **gestio, gestire, gestivi, gestitum,** throw oneself about, be cheerful about, long for

53

This anecdote in hendecasyllabic meter compliments the eloquence of Catullus' friend Licinius Calvus, who was noted for his prosecution of Vatinius. It is impossible to determine from the text whether Calvus' speech of 58 or 54 B.C. is referenced. The clever wit of Catullus animates the poem.

> Risi nescio quem modo e corona,
> qui, cum mirifice Vatiniana
> meus crimina Calvos explicasset,
> admirans ait haec manusque tollens,
> 'di magni, salaputium disertum!'　　　　　5

---

1 risi: **rideo, ridere, risi, risum,** laugh
nescio: **nescio, nescire, nescivi, nescitum,** not to know, be ignorant of; with the indefinite
　　　pronoun **quem:** someone (or other)
modo: **modo,** adv., just, now, only recently
corona: **corona, -ae,** f., a circle of bystanders at a trial

2 mirifice: **mirifice,** adv., wonderfully, exceedingly
Vatiniana: **Vatinianus-a-um,** adj., of or belonging to a certain Vitinius, whose name became
　　　associated with disrepute after prosecutions by Cicero and Calvus

3 **Calvos = Calvus:** prosecutor of Vatinius

5 salaputium: **salaputium, -ii,** n., midget
disertum: **disertus-a-um,** adj., eloquent, clever in speaking

62
LINES 1—19

This marriage poem, an *epithalamium*, is based in part upon earlier Hellenistic models. These wedding poems, written by Greek poets between the fourth and first centuries B.C., were usually tied to a specific mythological wedding. This poem offers a generalized re-enactment of the song contest between a group of girls and boys, who, while at an idealized wedding feast in the house of the bride's father, are now awaiting the arrival of the bride. The meter is dactylic hexameter.

Boys
> Vesper adest, iuvenes, consurgite: Vesper Olympo
> exspectata diu vix tandem lumina tollit.
> surgere iam tempus, iam pinguis linquere mensas,
> iam veniet virgo, iam dicetur hymenaeus.
> Hymen O Hymenaee, Hymen ades O Hymenaee!   5

Girls
> Cernitis, innuptae, iuvenes? consurgite contra;
> nimirum Oetaeos ostendit Noctifer ignes.
> sic certest; viden ut perniciter exsiluere?
> non temere exsiluere, canent quod vincere par est.
> Hymen O Hymenaee, Hymen ades O Hymenaee!   10

Boys
> Non facilis nobis, aequales, palma parata est;
> aspicite, innuptae secum ut meditata requirunt.
> non frustra meditantur: habent memorabile quod sit;
> nec mirum, penitus quae tota mente laborant.
> nos alio mentes, alio divisimus aures;   15
> iure igitur vincemur: amat victoria curam.
> quare nunc animos saltem convertite vestros;
> dicere iam incipient, iam respondere decebit.
> Hymen O Hymenaee, Hymen ades O Hymenaee!

---

1   **Vesper: Vesper, Vesperis,** m., evening-star
consurgite: consurgo, consurgere, consurrexi, consurrectum, rise, stand up

2   **vix: vix,** adv., scarcely, just now
tandem: tandem, adv., finally
lumina: lumen, luminis, n., eye, light
tollit: tollo, tollere, sustuli, sublatum, raise, lift

3   **pinguis: pinguis-pingue,** adj., rich, lavish, splendid
linquere: linquo, linquere, liqui, leave, depart

4   **hymenaeus: hymenaeus, -i,** m., wedding song

5   **Hymen: Hymen, Hymenis,** m., god of marriage

6   **innuptae: innupta, -ae**, f., unmarried girl, maiden
      contra: contra, adv., on the other side

7   **nimirum: nimirum**, adv., no doubt, certainly, of course
      Oetaeos: Oetaeus-a-um, adj., Oetean, Herculean; of or belonging to the Oetean mountain
         range between Thessaly and Aetolia, where Hercules ascended the funeral pyre
      Noctifer: noctifer, noctiferi, m., night-star

8   **certest = certum est**
      viden = videsne: this singular form should be translated as if it is plural.
      perniciter: perniciter, adv., nimbly, swiftly, quickly
      exsiluere: exsilio, exsilire, exsilui, spring out, bound forth

9   **non temere: non temere**, adv., not lightly, not easily, not rashly
      canent: cano, canere, cecini, cantum, sing
      par est: (an idiom) it is proper

11   **aequales: aequalis, -is**, m., comrade, friend
      palma: palma, -ae, f., palm of victory

12   **meditata: meditor, meditari, meditatus sum**, think over, reflect upon, practice
      requirunt: requiro, requirere, requisivi, requisitum, look for, search for, hunt for, demand;
         the sense seems to be "they seek out the things that have been studied."

13   **memorabile: memorabilis-memorabile**, adj., capable of being learned or memorized, re-
      markable

14   **mirum: mirus-a-um**, adj., surprising, amazing
      penitus: penitus, adv., internally, deep within

15   **alio . . . alio**: now here and now there
      divisimus: divido, dividere, divisi, divisum, divide, force apart
      aures: auris, -is, f., ear

16   **iure: ius, iuris**, n., law, right; **iure** means "rightfully."

17   **saltem: saltem**, adv., at least, in any event
      convertite: converto, convertere, converti, conversum, turn back

18   **incipient: incipio, incipere, incepi, inceptum**, begin
      decebit: decet, decere, decuit, it is fitting, proper, appropriate

62
LINES 20—38

Girls Hespere, quis caelo fertur crudelior ignis?　　　　20
qui natam possis complexu avellere matris,
complexu matris retinentem avellere natam,
et iuveni ardenti castam donare puellam.
quid faciunt hostes capta crudelius urbe?
Hymen O Hymenaee, Hymen ades O Hymenaee!　　　25

Boys Hespere, quis caelo lucet iucundior ignis?
qui desponsa tua firmes conubia flamma,
quae pepigere viri, pepigerunt ante parentes,
nec iunxere prius quam se tuus extulit ardor.
quid datur a divis felici optatius hora?　　　　30
Hymen O Hymenaee, Hymen ades O Hymenaee!

Girls Hesperus e nobis, aequales, abstulit unam.
* * * * * * * * * * * * * * * * * * * *　　(lacuna—break, lines lost)
* * * * * * * * * * * * * * * * * * *

Boys namque tuo adventu vigilat custodia semper,
nocte latent fures, quos idem saepe revertens,
Hespere, mutato comprendis nomine Eous.　　　35
at lubet innuptis ficto te carpere questu.
quid tum, si carpunt, tacita quem mente requirunt?
Hymen O Hymenaee, Hymen ades O Hymenaee!

20　**Hespere = Vespere; Hesperus** is the Greek name for the evening star.
caelo: ablative of place where, with the preposition unexpressed

21　**natam: nata, -ae**, f., daughter
complexu: complexus, -us, m., embrace
avellere: avello, avellere, avulsi, avulsum, tear away, remove, separate by violence

23　**ardenti: ardens, ardentis**, adj., passionate
castam: castus-a-um, adj., pure, chaste

24　**capta**: ablative modifying **urbe**

26　**lucet: luceo, lucere, luxi**, shine, shed light
iucundior: iucundus-a-um, adj., pleasant, agreeable, delightful, pleasing

27　**desponsa: despondeo, despondere, despondi, desponsum**, promise to give, pledge, betroth
firmes: firmo, firmare, firmavi, firmatum, confirm, strengthen
conubia: conubium, -ii, n., marriage

28 pepigere = pepigerunt: pango, **pangere, pepigi, pactum,** promise in marriage

29 iunxere = iunxerunt
ardor: **ardor, ardoris,** m., zeal, eagerness

30 felici . . . hora: ablative of comparison
optatius: **optatus-a-um,** adj., desirable, chosen, wished for

33 adventu: **adventus, -us,** m., arrival
vigilat: **vigilo, vigilare, vigilavi, vigilatum,** be on watch, on guard
custodia: **custodia, -ae,** f., watching, protection, guard

34 latent: **lateo, latere, latui,** hide
fures: **fur, furis,** m., thief
revertens: **revertor, reverti, reversus sum,** make one's way back, return

35 comprendis = comprehendis: **comprehendo, comprehendere, comprehendi, comprehensum,** catch hold of, seize
Eous: **Eous, -i,** m., morning-star

36 lubet = **libet, libere, libuit/libitum est,** it pleases, it is agreeable
ficto: **fictus-a-um,** adj., phoney, made-up, not true, false
carpere: **carpo, carpere, carpsi, carptum,** pluck, gather, wear away, chide, slander
questu: **questus, -us,** m., complaint

62
LINES 39—66

Girls
Ut flos in saeptis secretus nascitur hortis,
ignotus pecori, nullo convolsus aratro,   40
quem mulcent aurae, firmat sol, educat imber;
multi illum pueri, multae optavere puellae:
idem cum tenui carptus defloruit ungui,
nulli illum pueri, nullae optavere puellae:
sic virgo, dum intacta manet, dum cara suis est;   45
cum castum amisit polluto corpore florem,
nec pueris iucunda manet, nec cara puellis.
Hymen O Hymenaee, Hymen ades O Hymenaee!

Boys
Ut vidua in nudo vitis quae nascitur arvo,
numquam se extollit, numquam mitem educat uvam,   50
sed tenerum prono deflectens pondere corpus
iam iam contingit summum radice flagellum;
hanc nulli agricolae, nulli coluere iuvenci:
at si forte eadem est ulmo coniuncta marito,
multi illam agricolae, multi coluere iuvenci: 55
sic virgo, dum intacta manet, dum inculta senescit;
cum par conubium maturo tempore adepta est,
cara viro magis et minus est invisa parenti.
<Hymen O Hymenaee, Hymen ades O Hymenaee!>   58b *lines missing, supplied by context*

Girls
Et tu ne pugna cum tali coniuge, virgo.
non aequom est pugnare, pater cui tradidit ipse,   60
ipse pater cum matre, quibus parere necesse est.
virginitas non tota tua est, ex parte parentum est,
tertia pars patrist, pars est data tertia matri,
tertia sola tua est: noli pugnare duobus,
qui genero sua iura simul cum dote dederunt.   65
Hymen O Hymenaee, Hymen ades O Hymenaee!

---

39 **saeptis: saepio, saepire, saepsi, saeptum,** fence in, enclose
    nascitur: nascor, nasci, natus sum, be born
    hortis: hortus, -i, m., garden

40 **convolsus: convello, convellere, convelli, convolsum,** pull off, tear away, pluck
    aratro: aratrum, -i, n., plow

41 **mulcent: mulceo, mulcere, mulsi, mulsum,** soothe, appease, touch very lightly
    aurae: aura, -ae, f., breeze
    imber: imber, imbri, m., rain

43 tenui: **tenuis-tenue**, adj., fine, delicate, thin
carptus: carpo, carpere, carpsi, carptum, pluck

43 **defloruit: defloresco, deflorescere, deflorui**, shed blossoms, fade, droop
ungui: unguis, -is, m., fingernail

44 **optavere = optaverunt**
45 dum...dum = as long as...so long

46 **amisit: amitto, amittere, amisi, amissum**, lose
polluto: polluo, polluere, pollui, pollutum, defile, soil, violate

49 vidua: **viduus-a-um**, adj., barren, destitute, unmarried
vitis: vitis, vitis, f., vine, branch
arvo: arvum, -i, n., arable land, soil

50 mitem: **mitis-mite**, adj., ripe (sweet, juicy)
uvam: uva, -ae, f., grape

51 tenerum: **tener-tenera-tenerum**, adj., delicate, tender
prono: pronus-a-um, adj., bending, bent forward
deflectens: deflecto, deflectere, deflexi, deflexum, deflect, bend aside, turn away, bend down
pondere: pondus, ponderis, n., weight, burden

52 **contingit: contingo, contingere, contigi, contactum**, touch, come in contact with
radice: radix, radicis, f., root
flagellum: flagellum, -i, n., young vine shoot growing from the ground

53 **coluere: colo, colere, colui, cultum**, cultivate, till
iuvenci: iuvencus, -i, m., bullock, young bull

54 **ulmo: ulmus, -i**, f., elm tree
coniuncta: coniungo, coniungere, coniunxi, coniunctum, join together
marito: maritus, -i, m., husband

56 inculta: **incultus-a-um**, adj., untilled, unfertilized
senescit: senesco, senescere, senui, grow old, wither, become feeble

57 **adepta est: adipiscor, adipisci, adeptus sum**, obtain, get

58 invisa: **invisus-a-um**, adj., not wanted, a source of worry, being a burden, being distasteful

60 **aequom = aequum: aequus-a-um**, adj., fair, proper, balanced

61 **parere: pareo, parere, parui**, obey, yield to (with dative)

62 **virginitas: virginitas, virginitatis**, f., maidenhood, virginity

63 **patrist = patri est**

65 **genero: gener, generi**, m., son-in-law
sua: reference to the **parentum** of line 62
iura: ius, iuris, n., law, right
dote: dos, dotis, f., dowry

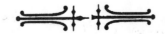

70

Catullus expresses frustration over the difference between what Lesbia says and what she does. This poem recalls similar sentiments expressed by the Greek poet Callimachus in his Epigram 25. Note that each poem henceforward is composed in the elegiac meter, which is regularly formed by one dactylic hexameter line and one dactylic pentameter line.

> Nulli se dicit mulier mea nubere malle
> quam mihi, non si se Iuppiter ipse petat.
> dicit: sed mulier cupido quod dicit amanti,
> in vento et rapida scribere oportet aqua.

---

1 nubere: **nubo, nubere, nupsi, nuptum**, marry, be wedded (with dative)
   malle: **malo, malle, malui**, prefer

2 quam: **quam**, adv., than

3 cupido: **cupidus-a-um**, adj., desiring
   amanti: **amans, amantis**, adj., loving; here an appositive, "lover"

4 oportet: **oportet, oportere, oportuit**, it is necessary

NB • mulier is a derogatory possessive
(if he respected her, he would use "femina")

72

This poem gives a specific example of the complaint voiced in Poem 70. The deepening levels of alienation within Catullus' relationship with Lesbia are unfolded as his anger is more vigorously demonstrated.

> Dicebas quondam solum te nosse Catullum,
>   Lesbia, nec prae me velle tenere Iovem.
> dilexi tum te non tantum ut vulgus amicam,
>   sed pater ut gnatos diligit et generos.
> nunc te cognovi: quare etsi impensius uror,   5
>   multo mi tamen es vilior et levior.
> qui potis est, inquis? quod amantem iniuria talis
>   cogit amare magis, sed bene velle minus.

---

1   **nosse = novisse = (cog)novisse**

2   **prae** (prep. + acc.): before

3   **dilexi: diligo, diligere, dilexi, dilectum**, love, esteem highly
tantum: tantum, adv., merely, only
ut: ut, adv., as
vulgus: vulgus, -i, n., common crowd, masses
amicam: amica, -ae, f., lover, ladyfriend, mistress

4   **gnatos = natos: nascor, nasci, natus sum**, be born; here "children," "sons"
generos: gener, generi, m., a son-in-law

5   **quare: quare**, adv., wherefore
etsi: etsi, conj., even if, although
impensius: impensus-a-um, adj., vehement, great, strong
uror: uro, urere, ussi, ustum, burn

6   **vilior: vilis-vile**, adj., vile, cheap
levior: levis-leve, adj., light, slight, trivial

7   **qui**, in the sense of "how"
potis: potis-pote, adj., able, capable
inquis: inquam, inquis, inquit, inquiunt, (defective verb) say

8   **bene velle: bene volo, bene velle, bene volui**, respect, wish well

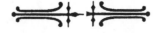

73

A further journey into relationships gone bad, the subject of Poems 70 and 72, this poem extends the poet's awareness of injustice and inequity. He seems to say that no matter how much loyalty he displays, it will not engender goodness in another person.

> Desine de quoquam quicquam bene velle mereri
> > aut aliquem fieri posse putare pium.
> omnia sunt ingrata, nihil fecisse benigne
> > \<prodest,\> immo etiam taedet obestque magis;
> ut mihi, quem nemo gravius nec acerbius urget   5
> > quam modo qui me unum atque unicum amicum habuit.

---

1   **desine: desino, desinere, desii, desitum**, give up, abandon; **velle** and **putare** are complementary infinitives governed by **desine**.
quicquam: accusative object of **mereri**
mereri: mereor, mereri, meritus sum, treat well, deserve; to be taken with **bene**

2   **fieri: fio, fieri, factus sum**, become, happen to be, be made

3   Although **ingratus** means ungrateful, the meaning here seems to be unrecognized or unappreciated; the ingratitude is manifested by lack of recognition or appreciation.
benigne: benigne, adv., kindly, gently

4   **prodest: prosum, prodesse, profui**, be useful, be profitable
taedet: taedet, taedere, taeduit/taesum est, it irks, it annoys, it wearies
obestque: obsum, obesse, obfui, be opposed to, be against, harm
magis: magis, adv., instead

5   **gravius: gravis-grave**, adj., heavy, serious
acerbius: acerbus-a-um, adj., bitter, harsh, sour
urget: urgeo, urgere, ursi, press, push, force, anger

6   The multiple elisions in this line provide an auditory and visual demonstration of the tight-knit bond which once existed between Catullus and his friend. This is an example of the iconic use of language, whereby the poet's chosen words essentially become a picture or enactment of a crucial idea being conveyed by the poem. The "pastness" of the relationship is also emphasized by the final word, **habuit**, a perfect tense form.

75

This poem portrays the poet's mind as so myopically preoccupied with Lesbia that he is unable to free himself from loving her whether she is bad or good.

> Huc est mens deducta tua mea, Lesbia, culpa
>   atque ita se officio perdidit ipsa suo,
> ut iam nec bene velle queat tibi, si optima fias,
>   nec desistere amare, omnia si facias.

---

1   **huc: huc,** adv., to this place

2   **officio: officium, -ii,** n., conscience, service, respect
      perdidit: perdo, perdere, perdidi, perditum, lose

3   **queat: queo, quire, quivi,** be able

4   The words **omnia si facias** mean "if you were to do everything imaginable." The implication
      is that if she were to do anything, no matter how terrible, he would still be unable to stop
      loving her.

76

This dramatic and poignant soliloquy shows the emotional struggle which Catullus undergoes as he tries to steel himself against continued association with Lesbia. The extreme urgency for a full break elevates this moment to one of life or death for the poet. There are many connections between Poems 76 and 73.

> Siqua recordanti benefacta priora voluptas
>   est homini, cum se cogitat esse pium,
> nec sanctam violasse fidem, nec foedere nullo
>   divum ad fallendos numine abusum homines,
> multa parata manent in longa aetate, Catulle,   5
>   ex hoc ingrato gaudia amore tibi.
> nam quaecumque homines bene cuiquam aut dicere possunt
>   aut facere, haec a te dictaque factaque sunt.
> omnia quae ingratae perierunt credita menti.
>   quare iam te cur amplius excrucies?   10
> quin tu animo offirmas atque istinc teque reducis,
>   et dis invitis desinis esse miser?
> difficile est longum subito deponere amorem,
>   difficile est, verum hoc qua lubet efficias:
> una salus haec est, hoc est tibi pervincendum,   15
>   hoc facias, sive id non pote sive pote.
> O di, si vestrum est misereri, aut si quibus umquam
>   extremam iam ipsa in morte tulistis opem,
> me miserum aspicite et, si vitam puriter egi,
>   eripite hanc pestem perniciemque mihi,   20
> quae mihi subrepens imos ut torpor in artus
>   expulit ex omni pectore laetitias.
> non iam illud quaero, contra me ut diligat illa,
>   aut, quod non potis est, esse pudica velit:
> ipse valere opto et taetrum hunc deponere morbum.   25
>   O di, reddite mi hoc pro pietate mea.

---

1   **siqua = si qua**: the **qua** modifies **voluptas**
       recordanti: **recordor, recordari, recordatus sum**, recall
       benefacta: **benefactum, -i**, n., good deed; this recalls the theme of Poem 73.
       voluptas: **voluptas, voluptatis**, f., pleasure

2   **homini**: dative of possession

3   **violasse = violavisse**: **violo, violare, violavi, violatum**, harm, injure, violate
       foedere: **foedus, foederis**, n., pact, agreement

4   **abusum**: **abutor, abuti, abusus sum**, use, abuse (with ablative)
       fallendos: **fallo, fallere, fefelli, falsum**, deceive, trick

9   The line recalls Poem 73. Here **omnia** is the subject of the verb **perierunt**; **sunt** is understood with **credita**.
perierunt: pereo, perire, perii, peritum, perish, die

10   **amplius: amplius**, adv., any further
excrucies: excrucio, excruciare, excruciavi, excruciatum, torture, torment

11   **quin**: (an interrogative particle) why not?
offirmas: offirmo, offirmare, offirmavi, offirmatum, be determined, steel oneself
istinc: istinc, adv., from there, from where you are

12   **dis = deis**
invitis: invitus-a-um, adj., unwilling, opposed

14   **verum: verum**, adv., in fact, truly
lubet = libet: it pleases

15   **salus: salus, salutis**, f., safety
pervincendum: pervinco, pervincere, pervici, pervictum, defeat completely, surpass

17   **misereri: misereo, miserere, miserui, miseritum**, feel sorry for; the verb, as in this instance, is also found in deponent form.
quibus = aliquibus

18   **tulistis: fero, ferre, tuli, latum**, bring, carry
opem: ops, opis, f., help, aid

19   **aspicite: aspicio, aspicere, aspexi, aspectum**, look at, notice
puriter: puriter, adv., cleanly, chastely, purely

20   **pestem: pestis, -is**, f., disease, plague
perniciemque: pernicies, perniciei, f., ruin, destruction
mihi: dative of separation

21   **subrepens: subrepo, subrepere, subrepsi, subreptum**, creep up to, steal upon
ut: ut, adv., as
torpor: torpor, torporis, m., numbness, grogginess

24   **pudica: pudicus-a-um**, adj., chaste, pure

25   **valere: valeo, valere, valui**, be strong, be healthy
taetrum: taeter-taetra-taetrum, adj., foul
morbum: morbus, -i, m., sickness, disease

26   The logic of this final plea recalls the thinking behind the opening lines of Poem 73.

77

This poem was probably addressed to Caelius Rufus, Clodia's new lover. The hostile sentiments which it expresses were likely occasioned when Caelius replaced Catullus in Lesbia's (Clodia's) affection.

> Rufe mihi frustra ac nequiquam credite amice
>   (frustra? immo magno cum pretio atque malo),
> sicine subrepsti mi, atque intestina perurens
>   ei misero eripuisti omnia nostra bona?
> eripuisti, heu heu nostrae crudele venenum   5
>   vitae, heu heu nostrae pestis amicitiae.

---

1   **Rufe:** Caelius Rufus of Cicero's *Pro Caelio*
       mihi: dative of agent with credite

2   Note the contrast between lines 1 and 2.

3   **sicine: sic** and **-ne; sic,** adv., thus; **-ne** showing a question: "is this the way?"
       subrepsti: syncopated form of **subrepsisti** from **subrepo, subrepere, subrepsi, subreptum,**
          creep up to, steal upon
       intestina: intestinus-a-um, adj., internal, personal; used substantively the word means "inner organs."
       perurens: peruro, perurere, perussi, perustum, burn up

4   Note the anaphora throughout this line and the poem in general.

5   **venenum: venenum, -i,** n., poison

83

Perhaps datable to the beginning of their relationship, this poem portrays Catullus and Lesbia situated together in the company of her unsuspecting husband. Catullus expresses amazement at how blind Metellus can be.

> Lesbia mi praesente viro mala plurima dicit:
>   haec illi fatuo maxima laetitia est.
> mule, nihil sentis? si nostri oblita taceret,
>   sana esset: nunc quod gannit et obloquitur,
> non solum meminit, sed, quae multo acrior est res,   5
>   irata est. hoc est, uritur et loquitur.

---

1   **mi = mihi**
    praesente viro: ablative absolute
    viro: Lesbia's (Clodia's) husband, Quintus Metellus Celer, who died in 59 B.C.

2   **fatuo: fatuus-a-um**, adj., stupid; here used substantively

3   **mule: mulus, -i**, m., mule
    oblita: obliviscor, oblivisci, oblitus sum, forget (with the genitive case)
    taceret: taceo, tacere, tacui, tacitum, be quiet

4   **sana: sanus-a-um**, adj., sane, rational; free from love
    gannit: gannio, gannire, snarl, growl
    obloquitur: obloquor, obloqui, oblocutus sum, speak, contradict, interrupt

5   **meminit: memini, meminisse**, (defective verb) remember, think of

6   **uritur: uro, urere, ussi, ustum**, burn, burn up
    loquitur: loquor, loqui, locutus sum, speak, talk

84

This humorous poem plays on the speech affectations of a certain Arrius, who insists on inserting the sound "h" in words that are not supposed to be aspirated. Catullus suggests that Arrius in fact has no speech problem, but instead is affecting an accent in a desperate attempt to sound sophisticated. He has not, however, succeeded in hiding his rather humble origins. Arrius may be Quintus Arrius, orator and friend of Crassus who went east in 55 B.C. The poem is a surprising contrast to its neighbors, which deal so dramatically with the changing emotional landscape of Catullus' and Lesbia's affair.

> Chommoda dicebat, si quando commoda vellet
>   dicere, et insidias Arrius hinsidias,
> et tum mirifice sperabat se esse locutum,
>   cum quantum poterat dixerat hinsidias.
> credo, sic mater, sic liber avunculus eius,   5
>   sic maternus avus dixerat atque avia.
> hoc misso in Syriam requierant omnibus aures:
>   audibant eadem haec leniter et leviter,
> nec sibi postilla metuebant talia verba,
>   cum subito affertur nuntius horribilis,   10
> Ionios fluctus, postquam illuc Arrius isset,
>   iam non Ionios esse sed Hionios.

---

1   Chommoda: commodum, -i, n., opportunity, advantage

2   insidias: insidiae, -arum, f. (plural), traps, ambush

3   mirifice: mirifice, adv., wonderfully

5   liber: liber-libera-liberum, adj., freeborn; implying servile lineage elsewhere in the family on the father's side
     avunculus: avunculus, -i, m., maternal uncle

6   avus: avus, -i, m., grandfather
     avia: avia, -ae, f., grandmother

7   requierant = requieverant: requiesco, requiescere, requievi, requietum, rest, repose

8   audibant = audiebant
     leniter: leniter, adv., softly
     leviter: leviter, adv., lightly

9   postilla: postilla, adv., afterwards
     metuebant: metuo, metuere, metui, fear

11   Ionios: Ionius-a-um, adj., Ionian, relating to the western coast of Greece
     illuc: illuc, adv., there, to that place
     isset: eo, ire, ii/ivi, itum, go, come

85

The themes of Poems 70, 72, 75, and 76 are compressed into this famous epigram. The extreme emotional torture which the poet is enduring is iconically represented by the elisions which create a balanced tonal contrast throughout. The opening question of line 1 is abruptly answered by the emotional declaration of line 2.

> Odi et amo. quare id faciam, fortasse requiris?
>   nescio, sed fieri sentio et excrucior.

---

1 **odi: odi, odisse, osus,** (defective verb) hate
quare: quare, adv., for what reason, why
fortasse: fortasse, adv., perhaps
requiris: requiro, requirere, requisivi, requisitum, seek, ask, ask for

2 **excrucior: excrucio, excruciare, excruciavi, excruciatum,** torment greatly, torture

86

The beauty and uniqueness of Lesbia emerge in this poem's curt dismissal of any attempt to compare her with an apparently attractive woman such as Quintia.

> Quintia formosa est multis. mihi candida, longa,
>   recta est: haec ego sic singula confiteor.
> totum illud formosa nego: nam nulla venustas,
>   nulla in tam magno est corpore mica salis.
> Lesbia formosa est, quae cum pulcherrima tota est,   5
>   tum omnibus una omnis surripuit Veneres.

---

1 **Quintia:** proper name of an otherwise unknown Roman lady
formosa: formosus-a-um, adj., shapely, beautiful
candida: candidus-a-um, adj., white, bright, fair, dazzling, gleaming
longa: longus-a-um, adj., tall

2 **recta: rectus-a-um,** adj., straight, well built
singula: singuli-ae-a, adj., one at a time, individually, one by one
confiteor: confiteor, confiteri, confessus sum, confess, admit

3 **venustas: venustas, venustatis,** f., beauty, charm

4 **mica: mica, micae,** f., crumb, morsel, grain
salis: sal, salis, m., salt, elegance, spice, wit

5/6 **cum . . . tum:** "not only . . . but also"

6 **surripuit: surripio, surripere, surripui, surreptum,** snatch secretly from, pilfer from. The elisions at the beginning of this line are iconic in that they present an audio-visual picture of many becoming one, essentially the sense which the poet attempts to convey here.

87

This poem, another assertion by the poet of his fidelity to Lesbia, verbally echoes Poems 70 and 76. *Nulla* in line 1 recalls *nulli* of Poem 70, line 1; *mulier* in line 1 recalls *mulier* of Poem 70, lines 1 and 3. *Foedere* in line 3 recalls *foedere* of Poem 76, line 3.

> Nulla potest mulier tantum se dicere amatam
>   vere, quantum a me Lesbia amata mea est.
> nulla fides ullo fuit umquam foedere tanta,
>   quanta in amore tuo ex parte reperta mea est.

1/2 **tantum . . . quantum**: as much . . . as
ellipsis of esse

2 **vere**: **vere**, adv., truly

3 **foedere**: **foedus, foederis**, n., pact, agreement, bond

4 **amore tuo**: in (my) love of/for you; the possessive adjective **tuo** is better translated here as if it were a personal pronoun in the genitive or dative case.
parte: **pars, partis**, f., part, share
reperta: **reperio, reperire, repperi, repertum**, find, discover, get, procure, realize

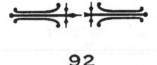

92

Reflecting the intensity of Poem 85 and using some of the vocabulary from Poem 83, this poem provides a window into the tortured soul of the poet.

> Lesbia mi dicit semper male nec tacet umquam
>   de me: Lesbia me dispeream nisi amat.
> quo signo? quia sunt totidem mea: deprecor illam
>   assidue, verum dispeream nisi amo.

---

2 **dispeream**: **dispereo, disperire, disperii**, go to ruin completely, be undone

3 **quia**: **quia**, conj., because
totidem: **totidem**, adv., just as many; the sense here seems to be "because things are the same with me," namely, "just as she keeps on talking about me and cannot keep quiet about me, so I cannot either stop talking or keep silent about my feelings for her."
deprecor: **deprecor, deprecari, deprecatus sum**, cry out, pray for relief, curse
illam: object of **deprecor**

4 **assidue**: **assidue**, adv., constantly

95

This poem, like Poems 22, 35, and 36, deals with the writing of poetry. Its theme is best expressed by the saying: quality not quantity, or perhaps "multum non multa."

> Zmyrna mei Cinnae nonam post denique messem
> quam coepta est nonamque edita post hiemem,
> milia cum interea quingenta Hortensius uno
> *
> Zmyrna cavas Satrachi penitus mittetur ad undas,   5
> Zmyrnam cana diu saecula pervolvent.
> at Volusi annales Paduam morientur ad ipsam
> et laxas scombris saepe dabunt tunicas.

---

1   **Zmyrna** was the title of a narrative poem by Cinna which told of the union of Cinyras and Zmyrna (Myrrha), from which came Adonis.
messem: messis, messis, f., harvest

2   **coepta: coepi, coepisse, coeptus,** (defective verb) begin
edita: edo, edere, edidi, editum, give out, put forth, publish

3   **quingenta** = 500; Hortensius was the well respected orator who may also have attempted to write some poetry.

5   **cavas: cavus-a-um,** adj., empty, hollow in the sense that the waves are deep-channeled
Satrachi: Satrachus, -i, m., the Satrachus, a river in Cyprus, perhaps connected with the stories told in Cinna's poem

6   **cana: canus-a-um,** adj., aged, old, venerable
pervolvent: pervolvo, pervolvere, pervolvi, pervolutum, keep reading through, keep turning over

7   **Paduam: Padua, -ae,** f., the city of Padua where perhaps Volusius, the subject of Poem 36, lived and wrote
morientur: morior, mori, mortuus sum, die

8   **laxas: laxus-a-um,** adj., loose
scombris: scomber, scombri, m., mackerel
tunicas: tunica, -ae, f., covering

95B

These two lines were probably a part of Poem 95 but were separated from the body of that poem in the manuscript tradition.

> Parva mei mihi sint cordi monimenta . . . ,
> at populus tumido gaudeat Antimacho.

---

1   **monimenta = monumenta: monumentum, -i,** n., memorial

2   **tumido: tumidus-a-um,** adj., swollen, long-winded
gaudeat: gaudeo, gaudere, gavisus sum, take delight in, take joy in (with dative)
Antimacho: Antimachus was a writer whose books seem not to have been very well respected in antiquity.

96

This is a touching composition in which Catullus tries to console his friend Calvus over the unexpected death of Calvus' wife, Quintilia.

Si quicquam mutis gratum acceptumve sepulcris
    accidere a nostro, Calve, dolore potest,
quo desiderio veteres renovamus amores
    atque olim missas flemus amicitias,
certe non tanto mors immatura dolori est   5
    Quintiliae, quantum gaudet amore tuo.

---

1   **mutis: mutus-a-um,** adj., mute, non-speaking
       sepulcris: sepulcrum, -i, n., tomb

2   **accidere: accido, accidere, accidi,** fall, happen, befall, develop
       Calve: the same Calvus addressed in Poem 50

3   **desiderio: desiderium, -i,** n., longing
       renovamus: renovo, renovare, renovavi, renovatum, renew, reawaken, revive

4   **flemus: fleo, flere, flevi, fletum,** cry, weep over, mourn for

5/6   The contrast rests upon **dolori** and **amore.** Simply expressed, the sorrow created by this
       untimely death is more than outweighed by the love which has characterized the relationship between Quintilia and Calvus.

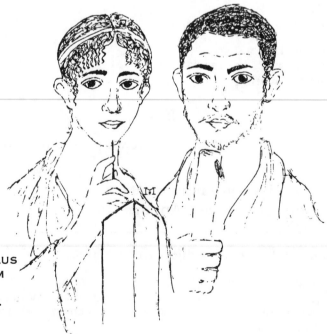

FRESCO OF
A. PAQUIUS PROCULUS
AND HIS WIFE, FROM
POMPEII,
FIRST CENTURY A.D.
LINE DRAWING BY
MALACHY EGAN.

101

Perhaps while in Bithynia in 57 B.C., Catullus visited the site of his brother's tomb. This poem, one of Catullus' most famous, is tenderly written and conveys the depth of the poet's feelings for his deceased brother.

> Multas per gentes et multa per aequora vectus
>   advenio has miseras, frater, ad inferias,
> ut te postremo donarem munere mortis
>   et mutam nequiquam alloquerer cinerem.
> quandoquidem fortuna mihi tete abstulit ipsum,   5
>   heu miser indigne frater adempte mihi,
> nunc tamen interea haec, prisco quae more parentum
>   tradita sunt tristi munere ad inferias,
> accipe fraterno multum manantia fletu,
>   atque in perpetuum, frater, ave atque vale.   10

1   **vectus: veho, vehere, vexi, vectum,** carry, transport

2   **advenio:** the use of the present tense adds poignancy and immediacy to this line, although imperfect subjunctives follow in secondary sequence.
      inferias: inferiae, -arum, f. (plural), rites or sacrifices in honor of the dead

3   **postremo: postremus-a-um,** adj., final, last
      donarem: dono, donare, donavi, donatum, present, grant, bestow

4   **nequiquam: nequiquam,** adv., pointlessly, in vain
      cinerem: cinis, cineris, m./f., cinder, ash

5   **quandoquidem: quandoquidem,** conj., in as much as
      mihi: dative of separation
      tete: intensive form of **te**
      abstulit: aufero, auferre, abstuli, ablatum, snatch away, steal, rob

6   **indigne: indigne,** adv., undeservedly
      adempte: adimo, adimere, ademi, ademptum, withdraw, take away

7   **prisco: priscus-a-um,** adj., ancient, pristine, beginning
      more: mos, moris, m., practice, custom
      parentum: parens, parentis, m./f., parent

8   **tradita: trado, tradere, tradidi, traditum,** hand down

9   **manantia: mano, manare, manavi,** be wet, be soaked
      fletu: fletus, -us, m., crying, tears

107

Catullus expresses his unanticipated joy at an impending reconciliation with Lesbia. The frequent repetition of words throughout the poem may indicate the poet's uncontrolled happiness.

> Si quicquam cupido optantique obtigit umquam
> insperanti, hoc est gratum animo proprie.
> quare hoc est gratum †nobis quoque† carius auro
> quod te restituis, Lesbia, mi cupido.
> restituis cupido atque insperanti, ipsa refers te   5
> nobis. O lucem candidiore nota!
> quis me uno vivit felicior, aut magis †hac est
> †optandus vita dicere quis poterit?

---

1   **cupido: cupidus-a-um,** adj., longing, desirous
     optantique: opto, optare, optavi, optatum, desire, wish
     optigit = obtigit: obtingo, obtingere, obtigi, happen, occur

2   **insperanti: insperans, insperantis,** adj., not expecting
     proprie: proprie, adv., properly, particularly

3   **†nobis quoque†:** daggers like these indicate an unreadable manuscript and tentative editorial solution.
     carius: carus-a-um, adj., dear

4   **restituis: restituo, restituere, restitui, restitutum,** restore

6   **lucem:** accusative in an exclamation; "O day with a more gleaming mark!"
     nota: nota, -ae, f., mark, sign, note

7   **felicior: felix, felicis,** adj., fortunate, lucky. Lines 7 and 8 have textual problems as indicated by the daggers before **hac** and **optandus.** The sense is best rendered if **res** is substituted for **est,** and, to modify it in the accusative plural, **optandus** becomes **optandas.**

109

The sadness of this poem recalls the tone of Poems 70 and 72. Here Catullus is apparently reflecting upon just how short of expectation his relationship with Lesbia has turned out.

> Iucundum, mea vita, mihi proponis amorem
> > hunc nostrum inter nos perpetuumque fore.
> di magni, facite ut vere promittere possit,
> > atque id sincere dicat et ex animo,
> ut liceat nobis tota perducere vita   5
> > aeternum hoc sanctae foedus amicitiae.

---

1   **iucundum: iucundus-a-um,** adj., pleasant
      proponis: propono, proponere, proposui, propositum, promise

2   **fore = futurum esse**

4   **sincere: sincere,** adv., honestly, sincerely

5   **tota . . . vita:** a rare ablative expressing duration of time

Meters

Catullus uses mainly the hendecasyllabic meter, occasionally the Sapphic, the iambic senarius and the limping iambics. In the long poems, Poem 61 uses pherecrateans and glyconics; Poems 62 and 64 are in dactylic hexameter; Poem 63 is in the galliambic meter; all the remaining poems (65–116) are written in elegiac distich. The metrical patterns of the meters used in this book appear below. The A. P. exam requires familiarity with the hendecasyllabic, Sapphic, dactylic hexameter, and the elegiac distich.

Hendecasyllabic

The hendecasyllabic is a meter composed of eleven syllables and five poetic feet. The name derives from the Greek word *hendeka* (eleven), from *hen* (one) and *deka* (ten). The first two syllables of the line may be an iamb (a short syllable followed by a long syllable), or a spondee (two long syllables), or a trochee (long syllable followed by a short syllable). The second foot is a dactyl; the third and fourth feet are trochees. The fifth foot can be either a spondee or a trochee. The final syllable can be long or short (syllaba anceps). The line is scanned as follows:

1	2	3	4	5
— —	— ᴗ ᴗ	— ᴗ	— ᴗ	— ᴗ̲
— ᴗ				
ᴗ —				

Iambic Senarius (Iambic Trimeter)

This meter appears in Poems 4 and 29 and consists of six iambs.

1	2	3	4	5	6
ᴗ —	ᴗ —	ᴗ —	ᴗ —	ᴗ —	ᴗ —

Limping Iambic

In Poem 31 the meter is essentially iambic, but there are variations. For example, the first and fifth syllables may be long or short, making the first and third feet either spondees or iambs; the last foot will be either a spondee or trochee. Such departures from the pure iambic senarius as seen in Poem 4 are usually identified as "limping iambs," "choliambics," or "scazons."

1	2	3	4	5	6
∪—	∪—	∪—	∪—	∪—	—∪
— —		— —			— —

Dactylic Hexameter

The meter of classical epic is the dactylic hexameter. This consists of six poetic feet comprising a maximum of 17 syllables. The fifth foot is almost always a dactyl and the sixth foot has two syllables forming either a spondee or a trochee. The final syllable can be long or short and is regularly called the syllaba anceps, the two-headed (doubtful) syllable. Any one or all of the first four feet of the hexameter line can become spondees. This meter is used in Poem 62 included in the A. P. syllabus. The normal scansion and the fully spondaic version appear below:

1	2	3	4	5	6
—∪∪	—∪∪	—∪∪	—∪∪	—∪∪	—∪
— —	— —	— —	— —	—∪∪	— —

Elegiac Distich (Couplet)

A meter which uses the dactylic hexameter line followed by a dactylic pentameter line is known as the elegiac couplet or distich. Poems 70 to 109 within the A. P. selections from Catullus follow this meter. The same variations which attended the hexameter line attend its use in this meter. The pentameter line, a line of five (not six) poetic feet, is really composed of two sections, each consisting of two and one half feet. The first part of the line can have two spondees followed by a long monosyllable. A caesura, the point where a breath is drawn by the reciter, is then inserted. The caesura is followed by two dactylic feet and a second monosyllable as is shown below. The two monosyllabic feet add up to one full foot, which, when added to the other feet, give five feet to the line.

1	2	3	4	5	6
Dactylic hexameter: −∪∪	−∪∪	−∪∪	−∪∪	−∪∪	− −

1	2	1/2		4	5	1/2
Dactylic pentameter: −∪∪	−∪∪	−	‖	−∪∪	−∪∪	∪
− −	− −					

Sapphic

The Sapphic meter takes its name from the Greek poetry of Sappho who wrote in the sixth century B.C. on the island of Lesbos. Catullus imitates one of her poems in Poem 51 but uses the Sapphic meter in Poem 11 as well. The meter is one based on quatrains. The four lines observe a pattern which shows two variations. The first three lines have eleven syllables each. These syllables are grouped in two pairs of four syllables around the three syllables of a dactyl. The fourth syllable and the eleventh syllable may be long or short. The scansion of the line can be trochee, spondee or trochee, dactyl, trochee, trochee or spondee. The final line is called an Adonic and consists of the last two poetic feet of the dactylic hexameter, namely a dactyl followed by spondee or trochee, since the final syllable is a syllaba anceps.

Lines 1–3:	1	2	3	4	5
	−∪	−∪	−∪∪	−∪	−∪
		− −			− −

Line 4 (the Adonic):	1	2
	−∪∪	−∪
		− −

Glyconic and Pherecratean

Poem 34 is composed of quatrains of three glyconic lines followed by one pherecratean line. The first two syllables can form a spondee, trochee, or iamb; a choriamb (long-short-short-long) and iamb follow to complete the line. A pherecratean is the same as a glyconic but there is one less syllable in the final foot. That final foot is monosyllabic, usually long but it can be short. Full scansion of these combinations are below:

Glyconic:

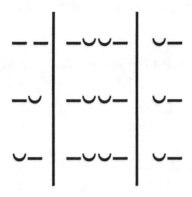

Pherecratean:

Figures of Speech

Figures of speech must not be confused with parts of speech. The latter define the type of word being used, such as a noun, pronoun, adjective, adverb, verb, participle, preposition, conjunction. Figures of speech are so called because their presence in a line of prose or poetry tends to shape the line by lending some subtlety of sound or sense which enhances the meaning of the line. The following list offers examples from the poems contained in this book. The student should be able to recognize and identify the figures, as well as offer an explanation of how the figures work in general and how the figures add to the meaning of the text or context in which they are found.

S

Alliteration: a series of words which begin with the same letter; subdivisions include consonance and assonance:

> miserunt mihi muneri Fabullus (Cat. 12.15)
> Note not only *miserunt* and *mihi,* but also *muneri.*

> cum suis vivat valeatque moechis (Cat. 11.17)
> *Vivat* and *valeat* begin with the same letter.

WO

Anaphora: repetition of the same word:

> O factum male! O miselle passer! (Cat. 3.16)
> Note the repetition of "O."

> da mi basia mille, deinde centum,
> dein mille altera, dein secunda centum,
> deinde usque altera mille, deinde centum. (Cat. 5.7–9)
> In this example *dein* and *deinde* are repeated for emphasis.

WO

Anastrophe: placing the object of a preposition before rather than after that preposition's occurrence in the line:

> oraclum Iovis inter aestuosi (Cat. 7.5)
> *Oraclum* is the object of *inter* but precedes it.

Antithesis: the side by side placement of words opposite in meaning; this may also be called **contraposition:**

> mutuis animis amant amantur (Cat. 45.20)
> The active and passive forms of the same verb are counterposed.

Apostrophe: the direct address of a person, place or thing as present when absent:

> Corneli, tibi: namque tu solebas
> meas esse aliquid putare nugas (Cat. 1.3–4)
> Cornelius is addressed and personalized when he is clearly not
> present.

> Amastri Pontica et Cytore buxifer (Cat. 4.13)
> The city of Amastris and the mountain Cytorus are addressed.

Assonance: repetition of similar vowel sounds either medial or final:

> tam gaudet in se tamque se ipse miratur (Cat. 22.17)
> Observe the repetition of *se* and its appearance in the word *ipse.*

> Advenio has miseras, frater, ad inferias (Cat 101.2)
> Note the repetition of *-as.*

Asyndeton: the absence of connectives between words, clauses, phrases:

> quicum ludere, quem in sinu tenere,
> cui primum digitum dare appetenti (Cat. 2.2–3)
> Notice that no connectives join the three relative clauses.

> sed obstinata mente perfer, obdura (Cat. 8.11)
> The two imperatives are not joined by a connective.

Chiasmus: an arrangement of pairs of words which, when written as separate lines, form the pattern A B B A; when lines are drawn connecting these common elements, the Greek letter X (chi) is formed; hence the term chiasmus denotes that formation:

>   a   b   b   a
> et acris solet incitare morsus (Cat. 2.4)
> *Acris* modifies *morsus, solet* governs *incitare.*

>   a   b   b   a
> quem plus illa oculis suis amabat (Cat. 3.5)
> *Illa* is the subject of *amabat; oculis* and *suis* modify one another.

>   a   b   b   a
> Caesaris visens monimenta magni (Cat. 11.10)
> *Caesaris* is modified by *magni; visens* governs *monimenta.*

Consonance: the repetition of the same consonantal sound medially or finally:

> lingua sed torpet, tenuis sub artus
> flamma demanat, sonitu suopte
> tintinant aures, gemina teguntur
>   lumina nocte. (Cat. 51.9–12)
> Note the use of the "t" sound throughout these lines, especially the onomatopoetic
>   *sonitu . . . tintinant.*

Ellipsis: the elimination of a word which is easily understood or derived from the context or from association with a nearby line:

> . . . meus sodalis—
> Cinna est Gaius, —is sibi paravit.
> verum, utrum illius an mei, quid ad me? (Cat. 10.29–31)
> Note the forms of the verb "to be" omitted in line 31.

Hendiadys: the use of two words with very similar meaning in order to assert one idea emphatically:

> vix mi ipse credens Thuniam atque Bithunos
> liquisse campos et videre te in tuto. (Cat. 31.5-6)
> *Thuniam* and *Bithunos campos* refer to the same place; by saying one the other is implied.

Homeoteleuton: a series of words which end in the same sounds:

> et quantum est hominum venustiorum (Cat. 3.2)
> The syllables *-tum, -num, -iorum* all end in the same sound"*um.*"

Hyperbole: extraordinary exaggeration:

> Verani, omnibus e meis amicis
> antistans mihi milibus trecentis (Cat. 9.1–2)
> Here Catullus suggests he has 300,000 friends.

Litotes: the assertion of something by denying its opposite:

> non sane illepidum neque invenustum (Cat. 10.4)
> The *non* qualifies *illepidum* and *invenustum*. The translation is then "not unadmirable or uncharming."

> si non illepidum neque invenustum est (Cat. 36.17)
> This is a repetition of the above in a later poem.

> Salve, nec minimo puella naso
> nec bello pede nec nigris ocellis
> nec longis digitis nec ore sicco
> nec sane nimis elegante lingua (Cat. 43.1–4)

Metonymy: the use of one word to suggest another:

> pleni ruris et inficetiarum (Cat. 36.19)
> *Ruris* means country and here suggests crudity.

Onomatopoeia: the matching of sound to sense:

> ad solam dominam usque pipiabat (Cat. 3.10)
> The verb *pipiabat* creates the sound of the bird's chirping.

> tunditur unda (Cat. 11.4)
> The sound of the wave pounding on the shore is recreated by *–und –*
> in the verb and the following word *unda*.

> loquente saepe sibilum edidit coma. (Cat. 4.12)
> The sounds of the initial "s" suggest the sound of breezes through
> the branches of the tree.

Personification: treating the inanimate as animate:

> Phaselus ille, quem videtis, hospites, /ait (Cat. 4.1–2)
> The boat is given the ability to speak.

> velim Caecilio, papyre, dicas (Cat. 35. 2)
> Catullus imagines that his papyrus has the ability to speak.

Polyptoton: repetition of key words with slight changes in the endings of the words:

> gemelle Castor et gemelle Castoris. (Cat. 4.27)
> Both the nominative and genitive forms of the proper noun *Castor*
> appear in this line.

> tam te basia multa basiare (Cat. 7.9)
> The noun *basia* appears as a cognate in the present infinitive *basiare*.

> ebrioso acino ebriosioris. (Cat. 27.4)
> Both the positive and comparative forms of the adjective are used.

Polysyndeton: the excessive use of connectives:

> Salve, nec minimo puella naso
> nec bello pede nec nigris ocellis
> nec longis digitis nec ore sicco
> nec sane nimis elegante lingua (Cat. 43.1–4)
> The connective *nec* is repeated numerous times above.

R   **Rhetorical Question:** a question which does not expect an answer:

> scelesta, vae te! quae tibi manet vita?
> quis nunc te adibit? cui videberis bella?
> quem nunc amabis? cuius esse diceris?
> quem basiabis? cui labella mordebis? (Cat. 8.15–18)
> Note the series of questions.

WO   **Synchysis:** an arrangement of pairs of words which forms the pattern A B A B; the parallel nature of the connection of these common elements leads to the term parallel word order:

>   a   b   a   b
> at mi nullus erat nec hic neque illic (Cat. 10. 21)
> In this example the correlative conjunctions *nec* and *neque* are
> associated, as are the adverbs *hic* and *illic*.

>   a   b   a   b
> Minister vetuli puer Falerni (Cat. 27.1)
> Here *minister* aligns with *puer* and *vetuli* modifies *Falerni*.

Sy   **Syncopation** or **Syncope:** the contraction of words such as the genitive plural of the second declension and the third person plural of the perfect indicative active:

> donarunt Veneres (Cat. 13.12)
> *Donarunt* is the contracted form of *donaverunt*.

WU   **Synecdoche:** a part of something which is used to suggest the whole (*pars pro toto*):

> neque ullius natantis impetum trabis (Cat. 4.3)
> *Trabis* means ship beam, which suggests ship.

R   **Tricolon:** grouping adjectives, nouns, phrases or clauses in threes:

> narrantem loca, facta, nationes (Cat. 9.7)
> Places, deeds, and nations form a tricolon.

WU   **Zeugma:** one word used simultaneously in both a literal and a figurative way:

> et me recuravi otioque et urtica. (Cat. 44.15)
> The verb *recuravi* means to heal emotionally (i.e., figuratively) by the use of *otio*,
> and to heal physically (i.e., literally) by the use of *urtica*.

CARPET-MOSAIC OF THE NINE MUSES, THIRD CENTURY A.D., FOUND IN TRIER, GERMANY.

Vocabulary

---------- **A** ----------

abhorreo, abhorrere, abhorrui, shrink back from, differ
abutor, abuti, abusus sum, use, abuse (with ablative)
accido, accidere, accidi, fall, happen, befall, develop
acer-acris-acre, adj., sharp, fierce
acerbus-a-um, adj., bitter, harsh, sour
acinus, -i, m., grape
acquiesco, acquiescere, acquievi, acquietum, become quiet, settle down
adimo, adimere, ademi, ademptum, withdraw, take away
adipiscor, adipisci, adeptus sum, obtain, get
adventus, -us, m., arrival
adversus-a-um, adj., opposite, facing
aequalis, -is, m., comrade, friend
aeque, adv., equally
aequinoctialis-aequinoctiale, adj., equinoctial
aequus-a-um, adj., fair, proper, balanced
aes, aeris, n., bronze, (by metonymy) profit
aestimatio, aestimationis, f., esteem, value
aestimo, aestimare, aestimavi, aestimatum, evaluate, rate
aestuosus-a-um, adj., sultry, very hot
aevum, -i, n., age, history
affero, afferre, attuli, allatum, bring, carry
ait: aio, (defective verb used mainly in present and imperfect) say
aliquis-aliquid, (indefinite pronoun) someone, something
amans, amantis, adj., loving
amarus-a-um, adj., bitter
Amastris, -is, f., Amastris, a city near Mount Cytorus
ambo-ae-o, adj., both
amica, -ae, f., lover, ladyfriend, mistress
amitto, amittere, amisi, amissum, lose
amnis, amnis, m., river
amo, amare, amavi, amatum, love, make love
amplius, adv., any further
animus, -i, m., mind, being
annalis-annale, adj., lasting one year
antique, adv., in ancient times
antisto, antistare, antistiti, (with the dative case) surpass, excel
anus, anus, f., old woman
appeto, appetere, appetivi, appetitum, seek, seek greedily, strive after
applico, applicare, applicavi, applicatum, hold, embrace
approbatio, approbationis, f., approval

Arabs, Arabis, m./f., an Arab
aranea, -ae, f., spider's web
aratrum, -i, n., plow
ardens, ardentis, adj., passionate
ardor, ardoris, m., flame of passion, zeal, eagerness
aridus-a-um, adj., dry
arvum, -i, n., arable land, soil
as, assis, m., a penny, a copper coin
aspicio, aspicere, aspexi, aspectum, catch sight of, look closely at
assidue, adv., constantly
assiduus-a-um, adj., continual
attingo, attingere, attigi, attactum, touch, come into contact with
attribuo, attribuere, attribui, attributum, allot, bestow
audeo, audere, ausus sum, dare
aufero, auferre, abstuli, ablatum, snatch away, steal, rob
aura, -ae, f., wind, breeze
aureolus-a-um, adj., golden
auris, auris, f., ear
auspicatus-a-um, adj., well-omened
auspicium, -ii, n., augury, the study of the flight of birds
autumo, autumare, autumavi, autumatum, affirm, assert
avello, avellere, avulsi, avulsum, tear away, remove by violence
aveo, avere, wish, want, desire strongly
avia, -ae, f., grandmother
avunculus, -i, m., maternal uncle
avus, -i, m., grandfather

B

basiatio, basiationis, f., a kissing
basium, basii, n., kiss
beatus-a-um, adj., happy, lucky
bellus-a-um, adj., beautiful, nice, cute, fine, lovely
bene volo, bene velle, bene volui, respect, wish well
benefactum, -i, n., good deed
benignus-a-um, adj., kind, gentle
brevis-breve, adj., brief, short
buxifer-buxifera-buxiferum, adj., producing boxwood trees

C

cachinnus, -i, m., loud laugh, a jeering
caco, cacare, cacavi, cacatum, defile, defecate
cacumen, -inis, n., extreme end of a thing, point, tip, peak
caeles, caelitis, m./f., heaven-dweller, god
caeruleus-a-um, adj., blue
caesius-a-um, adj., gray-eyed, blue-eyed

calix, calicis, m., cup, pot
candidus-a-um, adj., white, bright, dazzling, gleaming
cano, canere, cecini, cantum, sing
canus-a-um, adj., aged, old, venerable
caprimulgus, -i, m., a milker of goats
carpo, carpere, carpsi, carptum, pluck, gather, wear away, chide
carta, -ae, f., paper, a sheet of the Egyptian papyrus
carus-a-um, adj., dear
castus-a-um, adj., pure, chaste
caveto, second person singular future imperative of caveo, beware of
cavus-a-um, adj., empty, hollow
ceno, cenare, cenavi, cenatum, dine
certest = certe est
cinaedus-a-um, adj., shameless, crude
cinis, cineris, m./f., cinder, ash
circumsilio, circumsilire, hop around
coepi, coepisse, coeptum, begin
coetus, -us, m., meeting, crowd
cogitatio, cogitationis, f., reflection
cohors, cohortis, f., the staff, retinue
colloco, collocare, collocavi, collocatum, place, put in order
collum, -i, n., neck
colo, colere, colui, cultum, cultivate, till
comatus-a-um, adj., long-haired, leafy
commodo, commodare, commodavi, commodatum, lend, give, bestow
commodum, -i, n., opportunity, advantage
commodus-a-um, adj., favorable
comparo, comparare, comparavi, comparatum, procure, obtain, purchase
complector, complecti, complexus sum, embrace
complexus, -us, m., embrace
comprehendo, comprehendere, comprehendi, comprehensum, catch hold, grasp
confiteor, confiteri, confessus sum, confess, admit
coniungo, coniungere, coniunxi, coniunctum, join together
consurgo, consurgere, consurrexi, consurrectum, rise, stand up
contingo, contingere, contigi, contactum, touch, come in contact with
contra, adv., on the other side
conturbo, conturbare, conturbavi, conturbatum, confuse, disturb, upset
conubium, -ii, n., marriage
convello, convellere, convelli, convulsum or convolsum, pull off, tear away, pluck
convenio, convenire, conveni, conventum, be fitting, be proper, be agreed upon
converto, convertere, converti, conversum, turn back
conviva, -ae, m., guest, table companion
corona, -ae, f., circle of bystanders at a trial
credo, credere, credidi, creditum, believe
creo, creare, creavi, creatum, create, beget
cum, conj., when

cupidus-a-um, adj., desiring, longing, desirous of
cura, -ae, f., care, anxiety, love
curiosus-a-um, adj., inquisitive; (as a substantive) "busybody"
custodia, -ae, f., watching, protection, guard
Cyclades, Cycladum, f., the Cyclades Islands
Cyrenae, Cyrenarum, f., Cyrene, the capital of Libya
Cytorius-a-um, adj., pertaining to Mount Cytorus
Cytorus, -i, m., Mount Cytorus in Asia Minor

D

decet, decere, decuit, it is becoming, it is suitable, it does seem proper
decoctor, decoctoris, m., bankrupt, spendthrift
deferro, deferre, detuli, delatum, bring down, carry down
deflecto, deflectere, deflexi, deflexum, deflect, bend aside, turn away
defloresco, deflorescere, deflorui, shed blossoms, fade, droop
dein, deinde, adv., then
delicatus-a-um, adj., cute, fancy, racy, dainty
deliciae, deliciarum, f. (plural), delight, "sweetheart"
Delius-a-um, adj., relating to the island of Delos
demano, demanare, demanavi, flow down
depereo, deperire, deperii, be desperately in love with
deprecor, deprecari, deprecatus sum, cry out, pray against
desiderium, -ii, n., longing
desino, desinere, desii, desitum, cease, stop, give up, abandon
despondeo, despondere, despondi, desponsum, pledge, betroth
despuo, despuere, despui, desputum, spit upon, show contempt for
destinatus-a-um, adj., be fixed, determined in mind
devoro, devorare, devoravi, devoratum, devour, destroy
dicax, dicacis, adj., witty, sharp, sarcastic
differtus-a-um, adj., full of
digitus, -i, m., finger; **primus digitus,** fingertip of the index finger, forefinger
diligo, diligere, dilexi, dilectum, love, esteem highly
dirigo, dirigere, direxi, directum, make straight, level
disertus-a-um, adj., articulate, eloquent, clever in speaking
dispereo, disperire, disperii, go to ruin completely, be undone
divido, dividere, divisi, divisum, divide, force apart
do, dare, dedi, datum, give
doceo, docere, docui, doctum, teach
doctus-a-um, adj., learned
doleo, dolere, dolui, dolitum, grieve
dolor, doloris, m., grief, pain
dono, donare, donavi, donatum, give, dedicate, present, grant, bestow
dormio, dormire, dormivi or **dormii, dormitum,** sleep
dos, dotis, f., dowry
dulcis-dulce, adj., sweet

E

ebriosus-a-um, adj., drunken

ebrius-a-um, adj., drunken

edo, edere, edidi, editum, bring forth, give out, put forth, publish

edo, edere, edi, esum, consume

egelidus-a-um, adj., moderately warm

ei, (injection which governs the dative) alas

electus-a-um, adj., select, picked

elegans, elegantis, adj., elegant, charming, pleasing, rewarding

eo, ire, ii/ivi, itum, go, come

Eous, -i, m., morning-star

Eous-a-um, adj., eastern

error, erroris, m., wandering, wavering, flaw

erus, -i, m., heir, master of the house, owner

etsi, conj., even if, although

excrucio, excruciare, excruciavi, excruciatum, torment, torture

expello, expellere, expuli, expulsum, drive out, drive away, eject

expleo, explere, explevi, expletum, fill

explico, explicare, explicavi, explicatum, unfold, explain

expolio, expolire, expolivi, expolitum, smooth off, polish

exsilio, exsilire, exsilui, spring out, bound forth

exspecto, exspectare, exspectavi, exspectatum, expect, wait for

exsulto, exsultare, exsultavi, exsultatum, revel in, boast about

F

face, an imperative form of **facio**

faceret pili: non facere pili, an idiom meaning to care nothing about

facetiae, -arum, f., clever talk, humor

facio, facere, feci, factum, make, do

Falernus-a-um, adj., Falernian, from a region in Campania

fallo, fallere, fefelli, falsum, deceive, trick, cheat

fascino, fascinare, fascinavi, fascinatum, cast an evil eye upon, jinx

fatuus-a-um, adj., stupid

faveo, favere, favi, fautum, favor, promote

felix, felicis, adj., fortunate, lucky

fero, ferre, tuli, latum, bring, carry

fictus-a-um, adj., phoney, made-up, not true, false

fio, fieri, factus sum, happen, take place, be made, prove to be

firmo, firmare, firmavi, firmatum, confirm, strengthen

flagellum, -i, n., young vine or shoot growing from the ground

fleo, flere, flevi, fletum, cry, weep over, mourn for

fletus, -us, m., crying, tears

flos, floris, m., flower

foedus, foederis, n., pact, agreement, bond

fore = futurum esse

fores = esses
foret = esset
formosus-a-um, adj., shapely, beautiful
fortasse, adv., perhaps
fossor, fossoris, m., digger, lout, clown
frango, frangere, fregi, fractum, break
fretum, -i, n., strait, sound, channel
frux, frugis, f., fruit, produce
fuere = fuerunt
fugio, fugere, fugi, fugitum, flee
fui libenter, idiomatic for "I was delighted"
fulgeo, fulgere, fulsi, shine
fundus, -i, m., a piece of land, a farm, an estate
fur, furis, m., thief
furtivus-a-um, adj., stolen, secret, hidden
furtum, -i, n., theft

––––––––––––––––––––––––– **G** –––––––––––––––––––––––––

gannio, gannire, snarl, growl
gaudeo, gaudere, gavisus sum, rejoice at, find joy in (with dative)
geminus-a-um, adj., twin, both
gener, generi, m., son-in-law
gestio, gestire, gestivi, gestitum, throw oneself about, be cheerful, be excited
(g)nati, -orum, m. children [from **(g)nascor,** be born], "sons"
grabatus, -i, m., cot, asmall bed, couch
gradior, gradi, gressus sum, go, journey
gratum est, it is pleasing
gravedo, gravedinis, f., cold, head cold
gravis-grave, adj., serious, dire, grave
gremium, -ii, n., lap

––––––––––––––––––––––––– **H** –––––––––––––––––––––––––

habe tibi, an abrupt, colloquial phrase: "Take it in 'as-is' condition"
Hadriaticum, -i, n., Adriatic Sea
harena, -ae, f., sand, grain of sand
harundinosus-a-um, adj., overgrown with reeds
Hespere = Vespere
hesternus-a-um, adj., yesterday
Hiber, Hiberis, m./f., an Iberian or Spaniard
Hiberi, -orum, m., the Iberians or Spaniards
Hiberus-a-um, adj., Iberian, Spanish
hortus, -i, m., garden
huc, adv., to this place
Hymen, Hymenis, m., god of marriage
Hymenaeus, -i, m., wedding song
Hyrcani, -orum, m., people living on the shores of the Caspian Sea

I

iaceo, iacere, iacui, iacitum, lie, recline
idem, (used as an adv.), in the same way, likewise
identidem, adv., again and again, constantly
ignosco, ignoscere, ignovi, ignotum, pardon, forgive, have sympathy for
ilia, ilium, n. (plural), the groin
ille-illa-illud, (demonstrative pronoun/adjective) that
illepidus-a-um, adj., inelegant
illinc, adv., from there, on that side
illuc, adv., there, to that place
imber, imbris, m., rain
imbuo, imbuere, imbui, imbutum, wet, soak, saturate
immerens, immerentis, adj., undeserving
immo, adv., no, on the contrary
impensus-a-um, adj., vehement, excessive, great, strong
impotens, impotentis, adj., powerless to control, feeble, weak
incensus-a-um, adj., inflamed, burned up, set on fire
incido, incidere, incidi, incasum, fall upon, come unexpectedly upon
incipio, incipere, incepi, inceptum, begin
incohatus-a-um, adj., begun (not finished)
incoho, incohare, incohavi, incohatum, begin
incolumis-incolume, adj., unharmed, uninjured
incultus-a-um, adj., untilled, unfertilized
indignus-a-um, adj., unworthy
indomitus-a-um, adj., untamed, wild
ineptio, ineptire, make a fool of oneself
ineptus-a-um, adj., foolish
infacetus-a-um, adj., dull, not witty
infelix, infelicis, adj., sterile, unlucky
inferiae, -arum, f. (plural), sacrifices in honor of the dead
inficetiae, -arum, f., coarse jokes
ingero, ingerere, ingessi, ingestum, pour into
inicio, inicere, inieci, iniectum, throw on, cast on
innupta, -ae, f., unmarried girl, maiden
inquam, inquis, inquit, inquiunt, (defective verb) say
insidiae, -arum, f. (plural), traps, ambush
insperans, insperantis, adj., not expecting
insulsus-a-um, adj., tasteless, insipid
integer-integra-integrum, adj., chaste
intestinus-a-um, adj., internal, personal
invenustus-a-um, adj., uncharming; the antithesis of anything tastefully done
invideo, invidere, invidi, invisum, cast an evil eye upon
invisus-a-um, adj., not wanted
invitus-a-um, adj., unwilling, opposed

iocor, iocari, iocatus sum, tease, joke
iocosus-a-um, adj., humorous, funny
iocus, -i, m., jest, joke
Ionius-a-um, adj., Ionian, relating to the sea west of Greece
ipse-ipsa-ipsum, (intensive pronoun) -self
irrumator, irrumatoris, m., a deviate, pervert
istinc, adv., from there, from where you are
iucundus-a-um, adj., pleasant, agreeable, delightful, pleasing
ius, iuris, n., law, right
iuvencus, -i, m., bullock, young bull

L

labellum, -i, n., little lip
laboriosus-a-um, adj., labored over, worked
lacus, -us, m., lake, pond
laedo, laedere, laesi, laesum, offend, hurt, knock, strike
lar, laris, m., household god; (by metonomy) hearth, dwelling, home
Larius-a-um, adj., of or belonging to Lake Como
lasarpicifer-lasarpicifera-lasarpiciferum, adj., bearing or producing asafoetida,
    (loosely translated) "exotic"
lateo, latere, latui, hide
Latonia, daughter of Latona (Leto), i.e., Diana (Artemis)
laxus-a-um, adj., loose
lectica, -ae, f., litter
lectulus, -i, small couch, cot
lectus, -i, m., bed
lego, legere, legi, lectum, read, pick, traverse
lenis-lene, adj., gentle, soft
lepidus-a-um, adj., elegant, charming
lepor, leporis, m., pleasantness, charm, wit
levis-leve, adj., light, slight, trivial
leviter, adv., lightly, a little
levo, levare, levavi, levatum, lighten, ease
libellus, -i, m., small book
liber-libera-liberum, freeborn
libido, libidinis, f., longing, fancy, inclination
Libyssus-a-um, adj., Libyan
licet, licere, licuit, it is permitted
lignum, -i, n., wood, firewood, writing tablet
ligo, ligare, ligavi, ligatum, tie up, bind
limpidus-a-um, adj., clear, bright, transparent
linquo, liquere, liqui, leave, abandon, depart
linteum, -i, n., linen cloth, napkin, sail
liquens, liquentis, adj., liquid, fluid, clear
litoralis-litorale, adj., belonging to the shore

litus, litoris, n., shore
longus-a-um, adj., tall
loquor, loqui, locutus sum, speak, talk
lorum, -i, n., strip of leather
lubet = libet, libere, libuit/libitum est, it pleases, it is agreeable
luceo, lucere, luxi, shine, shed light
ludo, ludere, lusi, lusum, play
lugeo, lugere, luxi, luctum, mourn, lament
lumen, luminis, n., eye, light
Luna, Diana's name when she is associated with the moon
lux, lucis, f., light
Lydius-a-um, adj., Lydian, Etruscan
lympha, -ae, f., water

M

---

magis, adv., instead, more
male, adv., badly
malignus-a-um, adj., stingy, malicious
malo, malle, malui, prefer
malum, -i, n., apple
malus-a-um, adj., bad, evil
maneo, manere, mansi, mansum, remain, wait
mano, manare, manavi, manatum, flow, drip, stream
mantica, -ae, f., knapsack
maritus, -i, m., husband
meditor, meditari, meditatus sum, think over, reflect upon, practice
medulla, -ae, f., marrow
mellitus-a-um, adj., honey-sweet
membrana, -ae, f., skin, parchment, possibly a sack for a manuscript
memini, meminisse, (defective verb) remember, think of
memorabilis-memorabile, adj., capable of being learned or memorized, remarkable
menstruus-a-um, adj., monthly
mereo, merere, merui, meritum, deserve, earn
merus-a-um, adj., pure, unmixed; can be used substantively to suggest unmixed wine
messis, messis, f., harvest
metior, metiri, mensus sum, measure, travel
metuo, metuere, metui, fear
mi = mihi
mica, -ae, f., crumb, morsel, grain
migro, migrare, migravi, migratum, depart
milies, adv., a thousand, innumerable times
minax, minacis, adj., threatening
minister, ministri, m., servant, attendant

mirifice, adv., wonderfully, exceedingly
mirificus-a-um, adj., causing wonder, wonderful
mirus-a-um, adj., surprising, amazing
misellus-a-um, adj., poor little (diminutive form of miser-misera-miserum)
misereo, miserere, miserui, feel sorry for
mitis-mite, adj., ripe (sweet, juicy)
mnemosynum, -i, n., memorial
modo, adv., just, now, only recently
moechus, -i, m., adulterer
molestus-a-um, adj., troublesome, annoying, irksome
mollis-molle, adj., soft, gentle
monimenta = monumenta: monumentum, -i, n., memorial
morbus, -i, m., sickness, disease
mordeo, mordere, momordi, morsum, bite
morior, mori, mortuus sum, die
moror, morari, moratus sum, delay
morsus, morsus, m., bite, peck
mos, moris, m., practice, custom
mulceo, mulcere, mulsi, mulsum, soothe, appease, touch very lightly
mulus, -i, m., mule
munus, muneris, n., gift
mutus-a-um, adj., mute, non-speaking
mutuus-a-um, adj., mutual

N

namque, conj., for, with the enclitic conjunction -que
nascor, nasci, natus sum, be born, develop, transpire
nasus, -i, m., nose
nata, -ae, f., daughter
nato, natare, natavi, swim, float
nefarius-a-um, adj., impious, abominable
neglegens, neglegentis, adj., careless, neglectful, relaxed
nepos, nepotis, m., descendant, grandchild, nephew
nequeo, nequire, nequii or nequivi, nequitum, be unable
nequiquam, adv., pointlessly, in vain
nescio quid, "I don't know why," "I don't know something (or other)"
nescio quis, someone (or other), I don't know whom
nescio, nescire, nescivi, nescitum, not know, be ignorant of
Nicaea, -ae, f., capital city of Bithynia
Nilus, -i, m., the Nile river
nimirum, adv., no doubt, certainly, of course, surely, clearly
niteo, nitere, nitui, shine, be bright
noctifer, noctiferi, m., night-star
nolo, nolle, nolui, not wish; (imperative with a following infinitive) "don't"
non nimis, adv., not particularly

non temere, adv., not lightly, not easily, not rashly
norat = noverat, syncopated pluperfect active form of nosco
nosco, noscere, novi, notum, know, be acquainted with
nosti = novisti, syncopated perfect active form of nosco
nostrum, of us (genitive plural of the first personal pronoun)
nota, -ae, f., mark, sign, note
nothus-a-um, adj., not genuine, false, phoney, "pale"
nox, noctis, f., night, darkness
nubo, nubere, nupsi, nuptum, marry, be wedded to (with dative)
nugae, -arum, f., (plural) nothings, nonsense, trifles
numerus, -i, m., meter, measure, number

—————————————— O ——————————————

obduro, obdurare, obduravi, obduratum, persist, stick it out
obliviscor, oblivisci, oblitus sum, forget (with the genitive case)
obloquor, obloqui, oblocutus sum, speak, contradict, interrupt, chide
obstinatus-a-um, adj., resolute, determined, fixed
obsum, obesse, obfui, be opposed to, be against, harm
obtingo, obtingere, obtigi, happen, occur
obvius-a-um, adj., meeting with (with dative)
occido, occidere, occidi, occasum, set, fall down
ocellus, -i, m., eye, "jewel"
oculus, -i, m., eye
odi, odisse, osum, (defective verb) hate
Oetaeus-a-um, adj., Oetean, Herculean
officium, -ii, n., conscience, duty
offirmo, offirmare, offirmavi, offirmatum, be determined
olfacio, olfacere, olfeci, olfactum, to smell
oliva, -ae, f., olive, olive tree
opera, -ae, f., work, deed
oportet, oportere, oportuit, it is necessary
ops, opis, f., power, help, aid
optatus-a-um, adj., desirable, chosen, wished for
opto, optare, optavi, optatum, desire, wish
opus foret, from opus esse, (idiom) there is need of
orac(u)lum, orac(u)li, n., oracle
Orcus, -i, m., name of the god of the underworld
os, oris, n., mouth
otiosus-a-um, adj., at leisure, relaxing
otium, -ii, n., free time, ease, leisure

—————————————— P ——————————————

Padua, -ae, f., the city of Padua
palimpsestum, -i, n., an erased and reused manuscript
palma, -ae, f., palm of victory

palmula, -ae, f., little oar, oar blade

pango, pangere, pepigi, pactum, promise in marriage, agree

papyrus, -i, m./f., papyrus

papyrum, -i, n., papyrus

par est, (an idiom) it is proper

parens, parentis, m./f., parent

pareo, parere, parui, obey, yield to (with dative)

pars, partis, f., part, share

Parthi, -orum, m., Parthians, people living in Parthia

passer, passeris, m., sparrow

patronus/a, -i/ae, m./f., patron

paulum, adv., a little while

peccatum, -i, n., slip, fault, mistake

penetro, penetrare, penetravi, penetratum, enter, get to, penetrate

penitus, adv., internally, deep within

perditus-a-um, adj., ruined, lost, reckless

perdo, perdere, perdidi, perditum, destroy, ruin, lose

peregrinus-a-um, adj., foreign

perennis-perenne, adj., unending, enduring

pereo, perire, perii, peritum, be desperately in love, perish, die

perfero, perferre, pertuli, perlatum, carry through, endure, put up

pernicies, -ei, f., ruin

perniciter, adv., nimbly, swiftly, quickly

pernix, pernicis, adj., swift

pernumero, pernumerare, pernumeravi, pernumeratum, count up

peruro, perurere, perussi, perustum, burn up

pervinco, pervincere, pervici, pervictum, defeat completely, surpass

pervolvo, pervolvere, pervolvi, pervolutum, keep reading or turning over

pes, pedis, m., foot, foot of a sail, leg of a couch

pestilentia, -ae, f., plague, sickness, unwholesome atmosphere

pestis, -is, f., disease, plague

petitor, petitoris, m., candidate

phaselus, -i, m., a Greek word meaning a kind of ship

Phrygii campi = Bithyni campi

pignus, pignoris, n., pledge, token

pinguis-pingue, adj., rich, lavish, splendid

pipio, pipiare or **pipire, pipiavi, pipiatum,** chirp

plenus-a-um, adj., full of (with genitive)

plumbum, -i, n., lead

plus, pluris, adj., more

poema, poematis, n., poem (a Greek noun)

polluo, polluere, pollui, pollutum, defile, soil, violate

pondus, ponderis, n., weight, burden

porro, adv., further, on and on

possum, posse, potui, be able

postilla, adv., afterwards
postremus-a-um, adj., final, last
pote = potest
potis-pote, adj., able, capable
prae (preposition with accusative), before
praesertim, adv., particularly, especially
praetereo, praeterire, praeterii, praeteritum, pass by, surpass
praetor, praetoris, m., governor
praetrepidans, praetrepidantis, adj., excited, eager, very nervous
pratum, -i, n., meadow
priscus-a-um, adj., ancient, pristine, beginning
probe, adv., well, properly, correctly
proficiscor, proficisci, profectus sum, set out, advance, walk away
progenies, progeniei, f., offspring
pronus-a-um, adj., bending, bent forward
propono, proponere, proposui, propositum, promise
Propontis, Propontidis, f., the Propontis, the Sea of Marmora
proprius-a-um, adj., proper
prosum, prodesse, profui, be useful, be profitable (with dative)
pudicus-a-um, adj., chaste, pure
puerpera, -ae, f., woman in childbirth
pumex, pumicis, m./f., lava-stone, pumice
puriter, adv., cleanly, chastely, purely
purpureus-a-um, adj., deep red
puto, putare, putavi, putatum, think, consider

---------------------- Q ----------------------

quaero, quaerere, quaesivi, quaesitum, seek, ask
quaeso, quaesere, quaesivi, quaesitum, seek, "I beg" or "please!"
qualiscumque-qualecumque, (interrogative/indefinite adjective) of whatever kind
quam, adv., as, than
quamvis, adv., however, as much as you please
quamvis, conj., although
quandoquidem, conj., in as much as, since
quantus-a-um, (interrogative adjective) how much?
quare, adv., for what reason, why, on account of which thing, therefore
quasso, quassare, quassavi, quassatum, keep shaking or tossing
queo, quire, quivi, be able
questus, -us, m., complaint
qui-quae-quod, (relative pronoun) who, which
quia, conj., because
quicumque-quaecumque-quodcumque, (indefinite adjective) whatever
quin, (interrogative particle) why not?
quingenti-ae-a, adj., five hundred
quis = aliquis, (indefinite pronoun) someone, anybody

quisnam-quaenam-quidnam, (interrogative pronoun/adjective) what
quisquam-quaequam-quidquam, (indefinite pronoun) anyone, someone
quisquis-quaequae-quidquid, (indefinite relative pronoun) whoever, whatever
quivis-quaevis-quodvis, (indefinite adjective) any, any at all
quot, (interrogative adverb) how many
quovis pignore contendere, (an idiom) bet anything upon

R

radix, radicis, f., root
ratio, rationis, f., reason
recipio, recipere, recepi, receptum, welcome into one's house
reconditus-a-um, adj., hidden, concealed
recordor, recordari, recordatus sum, recall
rectus-a-um, adj., right, straight-backed, well built
recuro, recurare, recuravi, recuratum, refresh, restore to health
reddo, reddere, reddidi, redditum, return, give back
redeo, redire, redivi or **redii, reditum,** return
refectus-a-um, adj., refreshed
refero, referre, rettuli, relatum, transfer, carry, bring back
reflecto, reflectere, reflexi, reflexum, bend back, turn back
renovo, renovare, renovavi, renovatum, renew, reawaken, revive
repente, adv., suddenly, at that instant
reperio, reperire, repperi, repertum, find, get, procure, realize
requiesco, requiescere, requievi, requietum, rest, repose
requiro, requirere, requisivi, requisitum, look for, search for, seek
resono, resonare, resonavi, resound, echo
respecto, respectare, respectavi, respectatum, look back upon
restituo, restituere, restitui, restitutum, restore
revertor, reverti, reversus sum, make one's way back, return
Rhodus, -i, f., island of Rhodes
rideo, ridere, risi, risum, laugh, smile
rubeo, rubere, rubui, be red, "bloodshot"
ruber-rubra-rubrum, adj., red, ruddy
rumor, rumoris, m., gossip, rumor
rumpo, rumpere, rupi, ruptum, break, burst
rursus, adv., again
rus, ruris, n., the country, fields
rusticus-a-um, adj., rural, rustic

S

Sabinus-a-um, adj., Sabine, of or belonging to the Sabines
sacculus, -i, m., little bag, purse, wallet, knapsack
sacer-sacra-sacrum, adj., sacred, holy, revered
saec(u)lum, -i, n., an age, a generation
saepio, saepire, saepsi, saeptum, fence in, enclose

Saetabus-a-um, adj., Saetaban, belonging to Saetabis, a town in Spain

Sagae, -arum, m., Scythians

sagittifer-sagittifera-sagittiferum, adj., arrow bearing

sal, salis, m., salt, elegance, spice, wit

salaputium, -ii, n., midget

salsus-a-um, adj., salty, witty

saltem, adv., at least, in any event

saltus, saltus, m., forest

salus, salutis, f., safety

salveo, salvere, salui, be healthy; imperative means "hail," "hello"

sane, adv., naturally, (with negatives) really, at all, fully

sanus-a-um, adj., sane, rational; free from love

sapio, sapere, sapivi, have a sense of, have knowledge of, be wise, have a taste of

Sapphicus-a-um, adj., of or belonging to Sappho

satis superque, enough and more than enough

Satrachus, -i, m., the Satrachus, a river in Cyprus

scelestus-a-um, adj., wretched, unfortunate

scio, scire, scivi, scitum, know

scitus-a-um, adj., knowing, shrewd, witty

scomber, scombri, m., mackerel

scortillum, diminutive of **scortum, -i,** n., prostitute, harlot

scurra, -ae, m., jester, comedian, man-about-town

sector, sectari, sectatus sum, chase, follow, run after

secundus-a-um, adj., favorable

semel, adv., once

seneo, senere, senui, be old, age

senesco, senescere, senui, grow old, wither, become feeble

senex, senis, m., old man, aging man

septemgeminus-a-um, sevenfold, seven-throated

Septimille, diminutive, vocative of Septimius

sepulcrum, -i, n., tomb, burial ground

Serapis, Serapis, m., Egyptian god of healing

sermo, sermonis, m., conversation

servio, servire, servivi, be a servant or slave to

severus-a-um, adj., harsh, conservative, strict, austere

sibilus-a-um, adj., hissing

siccus-a-um, adj., dry

sicine, adv., "is this the way?"

sicut, conj., just as

sidus, sideris, n., star

silesco, silescere, be silent, grow quiet

sincerus-a-um, adj., sound, whole, clean, untainted, sincere

singuli-ae-a, adj., one at a time, individually, one by one

sinus, -us, m., bay, curve, fold of a toga, lap

sodalis, -is, m., comrade, companion

sol, solis, m., sun
solaciolum, solacioli, n., a little comfort or solace
soleo, solere, solitus sum, be accustomed to, be used to
solvo, solvere, solvi, solutum, dissolve, break up, free
sono, sonare, sonui, sonitum, sound
sonitus, -us, m., sound
sordidus-a-um, adj., in poor taste, crude
sospito, sospitare, sospitavi, sospitatum, preserve, protect
stagnum, -i, n., standing or still water
sterno, sternere, sternui, sneeze, sputter
suavior (= savior), suaviari, suaviatus sum, kiss
suavis-suave, adj., pleasant, charming, agreeable
suburbanus-a-um, adj., suburban (situated near a city)
sudarium, -ii, n., handkerchief, napkin
sumptuosus-a-um, adj., very expensive, costly, lavish, extravagant
suopte = suo [from suus-a-um + pte (enclitic)]
subrepo, subrepere, subrepsi, subreptum, creep up to, steal upon
surripio, surripere, surripui, surreptum, snatch, pilfer from

---

T

tabella, -ae, f., board, writing tablet
taceo, tacere, tacui, tacitum, be silent, still
taedet, taedere, taeduit/taesum est, it irks/annoys/wearies
taeter-taetra-taetrum, adj., foul
talentum, -i, n., a talent, a sum of money
tandem, adv., finally
tango, tangere, tetigi, tactum, touch
tantum, adv., merely, only
tardipes, tardipedis, adj., slow-footed, limping
tego, tegere, texi, tectum, cover, protect
tenebrae, -arum, f., (plural) darkness (of the underworld)
tenebricosus-a-um, adj., dark, obscure, murky
teneo, tenere, tenui, tentum, hold, keep
tener-tenera-tenerum, adj., delicate, tender
tenuis-tenue, adj., fine, delicate, thin, tender
tepor, teporis, m., gentle warmth, lukewarmness
tete, intensive form of te
Thracius-a-um, adj., of or belonging to Thrace
Thyonianus, -i, m., son of Thyone, i.e., Bacchus
Tiburs, Tiburtis, adj., of or belonging to Tibur (Tivoli)
tintino, tintinare, tintinavi, ring, tingle
tollo, tollere, sustuli, sublatum, raise, lift
torpeo, torpere, torpui, be numb, be stiff
torpor, torporis, m., numbness, grogginess

torreo, torrere, torrui, tostum, roast, bake, burn
totidem, adj., (indeclinable) just as many
trabs, trabis, f., plank, beam
trado, tradere, tradidi, traditum, hand down
trecenti-ae-a, adj., three hundred
tres-tres-tria, adj., three
tristis-triste, adj., sad, miserable
trux, trucis, adj., savage, grim, fierce
tumidus-a-um, adj., swollen, long-winded
tundo, tundere, tutudi, tunsum, beat, pound, hammer
tunica, -ae, f., covering
turgidulus-a-um, adj., swollen
tussis, tussis, f., cough

──────────────── U ────────────────

uber, uberis, adj., fruitful
ulciscor, ulcisci, ultus sum, avenge oneself on, punish
ullus-a-um, adj., any
ulmus, -i, f., elm tree
ultimus-a-um, adj., last, final, farthest, edge of
umbilicus, -i, m., center dowels on which a book was rolled
unanimus-a-um, adj., of one mind, loving
unctus-a-um, adj., greasy, "slick"
unguentum, -i, n., ointment, perfume
unguis, -is, m., fingernail
unus-a-um, adj., alone, one
urbanus-a-um, adj., of the city/town, sophisticated, "city slicker"
urgeo, urgere, ursi, press, push, force, anger
uro, urere, ussi, ustum, burn, burn up
urtica, -ae, f., nettle (an herb)
usque, adv., continuously, without a break
ustulo, ustulare, ustulavi, ustulatum, burn a little, scorch
ut, (followed by the indicative mood) where, as
uter-utra-utrum, adj., which one of two
utor, uti, usus sum, use (with ablative)
utrum, adv., whether
uva, -ae, f., grape

──────────────── V ────────────────

vae, (interjection which governs the accusative or dative) alas, woe
vagor, vagari, vagatus sum, wander
valeo, valere, valui, be strong, be healthy
varius-a-um, adj., different
Vatinianus-a-um, adj., of or belonging to a Vatinius
vehemens, vehementis, adj., violent, impetuous

veho, vehere, vexi, vectum, carry, transport
velut, adv., just as
vemens = vehemens
venenum, -i, n., poison
venter, ventris, m., stomach (metonymy for greed or appetite)
ventito, ventitare, ventitavi, ventitatum, keep on going, keep following
venustas, venustatis, f., beauty, charm
venustus-a-um, adj., beautiful, charming, attractive
ver, veris, n., spring-time, youth
vere, adv., truly
versiculus, -i, m., small verse
verso, versare, versavi, versatum, turn
versus, -us, m., line of writing
verum, adv., in fact, truly
verus-a-um, adj., true, real
vesanus-a-um, adj., not of sound mind, insane
Vesper, Vesperis, m., evening-star
vetulus-a-um, adj., old
vetus, veteris, adj., old
vibro, vibrare, vibravi, vibratum, brandish, shake, flick
viduus-a-um, adj., barren, destitute
vigesco, vigescere, vigui, gain strength, become lively/vigorous
vigilo, vigilare, vigilavi, vigilatum, be on watch, on guard
vilis-vile, adj., vile, cheap
violo, violare, violavi, violatum, harm, injure, violate
virginitas, virginitatis, f., maidenhood, virginity
virgo, virginis, f., maiden, virgin
viso, visere, visi, visum, see, behold
vitis, vitis, f., vine, branch
vivo, vivere, vixi, victum, live
vix, adv., scarcely, just now
volo, velle, volui, wish, want
voluntas, voluntatis, f., wish, will
voluptas, voluptatis, f., pleasure
voro, vorare, voravi, voratum, swallow, devour
votum, -i, n., solemn vow
voveo, vovere, vovi, votum, vow
vulgus, -i, n., common crowd, masses

Z

Zephyrus, -i, m., west wind
zona, -ae, f., girdle

www.BOLCHAZY.com
—ENJOY LIVING LATIN—

Rome's Golden Poets

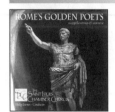

1000 Latin Proverbs

Vergil's Dido Opera

Schola Cantans

Carmina Burana

Latine Cantemus

How the Grinch Stole Christmas *in Latin*

Latin Music Through the Ages

The Cat in the Hat *in Latin*

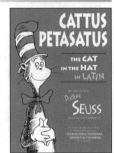

The Giving Tree *in Latin*

Shock-Headed Peter *in Latin*

"Yes, Virginia, there is a Santa Clause"...in Latin

Enrich Your Latin Learning

*Explore **bolchazy.com** for more on **Scholarship**, **Buttons**, the **Classical Bulletin**, **Responsible Popularization**, and **Living Latin***

—Order Online Today—